The Sinking of the
U.S.S. *Eagle PE-56*
Silent Victim of the *U-853*

*"The Greatest, Recently Solved Mystery in
New England's Naval & Maritime History"*

Paul Lawton

Dedication

This story is dedicated to the memories of the 49 brave, young U.S. Navy Officers and crewmen killed in action aboard the U.S.S. *Eagle 56* (*PE-56*) on Monday 23 April 1945, and to her 13 survivors; to the memory of my late uncle, U.S. Army (M4 Sherman) tank commander, Lieutenant John Henry Cashman, Jr. ('H" Company, 1st Armored Regiment, 1st Armored Division), who was killed in action at the Battle for Hill 609 in Tunisia, North Africa during "Operation Vulcan" on Friday 30 April 1943; and to my late father, Judge (Ret.) James Robert Lawton (10/20/1925 - 03/20/2007), formerly deployed with "I" Company, 503rd Parachute Infantry Regiment, 17th Airborne Division, U.S. Army, who was seriously wounded in action by a German Panther tank shell at the outskirts of Wessel, Germany during "Operation Varsity" on Friday 30 March 1945, and whose vital assistance was critical to the correction of the historical record of this chapter in World War II military history.

In Memoriam

Paul Blanchette, Jr., of Dracut, Massachusetts. One of the original members of the U.S.S. *Eagle 56* (*PE-56*) Search Team's Deep Dive Team, who, at the age of 49, lost his life on a training dive on the wreck of the tanker M/V Chester A. Poling off the coast of Gloucester, Massachusetts on Monday 18 May 2009. We finally found her, Paul!

Contents

Front Cover Photographs

(Top): The U.S. Navy, Ford Motor Company built Eagle class sub-chaser U.S.S. *Eagle 56 (PE-56)* at Newport News, Virginia in or about the mid to late 1920s. Courtesy of G. L. Johnson.

(Bottom): The Type IXC/40 W.W.II era German U-boat *U-853* on 23 February 1945 departing Stavanger, Norway on her second and final patrol of the war under command of Oberleutnant zur See Helmut Frömsdorf, with 55 Officers and crewmen aboard. Courtesy of the U-boot Archiv.

Back Cover Photographs

(Top Left): The U.S. Navy Officers and crewmen in formation on the stern of the U.S.S. *Eagle 56 (PE-56)*, during the Change-of-Command Ceremony at the Portland, Maine Navy Base on January 23, 1945, exactly three months to the day before the loss of the *PE-56*. Commander (Lt. Jg) John L. Barr, Jr. (standing center) reads the Change-of-Command Order, as he transfers command of the ship to Lieutenant Commander James G. Early (standing to the right of Captain Barr). Lt. Cdr. Barr requested a transfer to the Pacific theater to "see enemy action against the Japanese." Lieutenant John P. Scagnelli is standing to the right of Lt. Barr, facing left. Courtesy of John P. Scagnelli.

(Top Right): The Type IXC/40 W.W.II era German U-boat *U-853* at her Commissioning on 25 June 1943. Her original Commander, Kapitanleutnant Helmut Sommer is seen standing on deck, bottom row, 5th from the right with the white dress belt. Oberleutnant zur See Helmut Frömsdorf, is to the right of Commander Sommer, wearing a white dress belt and hanging ceremonial dagger. Courtesy of the U-boot Archiv.

(Bottom): The U.S.S. *Eagle 56 (PE-56)* engineering crew, or so-called "black gang" assembled on the stern of the ship at the U.S. Navy's Sound Training School at Key West, Florida, in or about May of

1944. Shown are: First row (front) kneeling, from left to right: Walter Goe; Harold Petersen; Oscar Davis; John Charles Merk; Shockley (aka "Bones") first name unknown; Novack, first name unknown. Second row (middle) standing, from left to right: Lieutenant John P. Scagnelli; Unidentified; John L. Breeze; Joseph Priestas; John A. Wisniewski; James Pemberton; Unidentified; Chief Robert Lemmon. Third row (rear) standing, from left to right: McDonald, first name unknown; Frederick Michelsen; Eliott Massey Shinn; Robert Petersen; Frank Ayers; Clark, first name unknown; Unidentified; Maurice Joseph Manning. Courtesy of John P. Scagnelli.

The Sinking of U.S.S. *Eagle 56* (*PE-56*): Silent Victim of *U-853* (23 April 1945)

In the final days of German belligerence during World War II, a little known chapter in naval history took place just off the American Northeast Coast, resulting in the greatest loss of U.S. Naval personnel in New England waters during the war, and one of the most enduring naval & maritime mysteries in United States history. The sinking of a small American warship, erroneously attributed by the Navy to a possible "boiler explosion," was followed by an extensive 12-day U.S. Navy hunt for the true culprit, leading to the destruction of a German U-boat, an American merchant freighter, and the loss of 116 American and German naval and merchant Officers and crewmen. For 56 years the story of the final patrol of the German U-boat *U-853*, and the loss of the U.S. Navy warship U.S.S. *Eagle 56* (*PE-56*) have been little more than footnotes in naval history, though the memories of the brave young Officers and crewmen who lost their lives aboard these warships continue to cry out for a full and complete accounting of their last days at war.

The United States Ship, Patrol Escort (Eagle Class) U.S.S. *Eagle 56* (*PE-56*), a so-called "Eagle Boat," was one of 60 late World War I era sub-chasers of the class. Constructed by the Ford Motor Company at its 1,700 foot long enclosed railway assembly line

River Rouge plant in Dearborn, Michigan, near Detroit, she was not commissioned until 22 October 1919, after the end of the war. The name for this class of vessel came from a 23 December 1917 *Washington Post* editorial calling for "an eagle to scour the seas and pounce upon every submarine that dares to leave German or Belgian shores." By Armistice Day (11 November 1918), only seven Eagle Boats had been completed and fitted-out, two of which had reached the Atlantic coast.

Her corvette-type hull was constructed of steel riveted flanged plate, she was 200 feet 9 inches long, had a 33 foot beam, 8 foot 6 inch draft, and displaced approximately 488 tons (615 tons fully loaded). She was powered by two Thornycroft-Bureau Express type, oil fired, three drum, water-tube boilers, equipped with duplex safety valves, and operating pressures of 250 psi. Steaming a single Poole manufactured geared turbine with 2,500 shaft horse-power turning a single screw, she had a top speed of 18 knots, and a range of 3,500 miles at 10 knots cruise speed. She was equipped with sonar, two 10 kilowatt generators and a 24-inch searchlight. For armament, she was originally fitted with one 3-inch/23-caliber anti-aircraft gun; two 4-inch/50-caliber Mark IX single-purpose deck guns; two .50-caliber Browning M2 heavy machine-guns; one Y-gun depth-charge projector aft; and two stern mounted depth-charge tracks, each containing ten 420-pound Mk6, or 520-pound magnetic Mk 8 "ashcan" depth-charges. By 1945 the *PE-56* had her Y-gun removed to accommodate target-towing gear and her aft 4-inch deck-gun had been replaced by a single .50-caliber machine-gun. Her original complement consisted of 5 Officers, 12 non-commissioned Officers and 56 enlisted men (78 total), though her complement was later reduced to 68, and ultimately to approximately 65 at the time of her loss.

The *PE-56* reached the North Atlantic via the Great Lakes, canals, and the St. Lawrence River. After arriving at the Portsmouth, New Hampshire Navy Yard in the spring of 1920, she was assigned to the District of Columbia Naval Reserve Force in November of

1921, where she conducted regular reserve training cruises from Chesapeake Bay to such ports as Key West, Florida, and Hamilton, Bermuda. In January of 1926 she was transferred to Baltimore, Maryland, where she continued duty as a Navy Reserve training ship before being transferred for refitting at Philadelphia for inshore patrol duty for the Fourth Naval District. The *PE-56* was one of only eight of the original 60 Eagle Boats to see service with the U.S. Navy during World War II.

In the early morning hours of 28 February 1942 the *PE-56* was dispatched from Cape May, New Jersey, to conduct rescue operations, after the 314 foot long, 1,090 ton, flush-deck, four-stacker Wickes-Class destroyer U.S.S. *Jacob Jones II (DD-130)*, under command of Lieutenant Commander, Hugh D. Black, Jr., was torpedoed and sunk by the German Type VIIC U-boat, *U-578*, under command of Korvettenkapitan, Ernst-August Rehwinkel, on the evening of the 27th. The wreck of the *Jacob Jones II* broke in half and went down in 125 feet of water at Latitude 38 degrees 41 minutes North; Longitude 74 degrees 29 minutes West, approximately 22 miles off the Delaware coast. A U.S. Army aircraft assigned to shore defense, and piloted by Army 1st Lt. L.R. Blackburn, Jr., located and circled the survivors, and directed the *PE-56* to the location of the *DD-130's* life-rafts. The *PE-56* located one of the destroyer's empty life-boats, and 20 minutes later she found a life-raft with 3 of the *Jacob Jones II's* survivors, along with the bodies of 4 dead crewmen. After taking aboard the survivors, the *PE-56's* Commander attempted to hasten the search for, and rescue of additional survivors, by taking the life-raft under tow. The raft soon broke up under the force of the tow, however, sending the 4 bodies to the bottom. Of the 101 Officers and crewmen aboard the U.S.S. *Jacob Jones II*, only 12 crewmen, no Officers, survived to be rescued by the *PE-56*, and one of the rescued crewmen (water-tender Carl Smith) later died en route back to Cape May. On 1 March 1942 the *PE-56* was again patrolling the area off Cape May, and conducted multiple depth-charge attacks on a sonar contact not far from where the U.S.S. *Jacob Jones II* had been torpedoed and sunk.

On 3 May 1942 the *PE-56* was again dispatched to conduct rescue operations, after a collision between two freighters at the mouth of Delaware Bay. The outbound 394 foot, 5,090 ton British Standard Transportation Co. Ltd. (formerly the 1925 built S.S. *Mobiloil 36*) freighter S.S. *Voco*, collided with the inbound 357 foot, 3,915 ton Canadian flagged British Gypsum Packet Co., Ltd. freighter S.S. *Gypsum Prince*, sending the smaller vessel to the bottom in 80 feet of water, with the loss of her Captain and five crewmen. Two U.S. Coast Guard picket boats rescued 20 men from the turbulent waters after the sinking of the *Gypsum Prince*, before the *PE-56* arrived on scene and recovered one body from the floating wreckage. Because the shallow wreck of the *Gypsum Prince* posed a serious menace to navigation at the busy entrance to Delaware Bay, the next day the *PE-56* returned to the scene to mark the obstruction with a navigational warning buoy. In doing so, the *PE-56* fouled her propeller on the dangerous wreckage, and had to be towed by the U.S. Navy tug U.S.S. *Allegheny* (AT-19), back to the Philadelphia Navy Yard for repairs.

On 24 May 1942 she departed Norfolk, Virginia, as a convoy escort to Key West, where she reported for duty as a sound training school-ship conducting exercises in anti-submarine warfare tactics. While in Key West the *PE-56* also took part in the development of the U.S. Navy's top-secret "homing mine," actually the passive acoustic homing Mark XXIV (Mk 24) "Fido" anti-submarine torpedo, by acting as an acoustic target during testing trials.

On 4 June 1944 she departed Key West for the Boston, Massachusetts Navy Yard where she underwent repairs before reporting for operations at the U.S. Naval Frontier Base at Portland, Maine, on 26 June 1944. At Portland, she spent the rest of her career towing targets consisting of an 18 inch diameter by 4 foot long cylindrical float. Painted green and called the "pickle" by the

PE-56 crew, the target was mounted on a sled and towed at the end of a 500 yard cable. The *PE-56* regularly towed this target in local operating areas off the coast of Cape Elizabeth for bombing target practice by U.S. Navy Grumman TBF "Avenger" torpedo bomber aircraft from the Naval Air Station at Brunswick, Maine.

On 23 January 1945 the *PE-56* conducted a Change-of-Command ceremony at Portland in which Captain (Lieutenant Commander) John L. Barr, , was relieved of command and replaced by Lt. Cdr. (LCDR) James G. Early, as Captain Barr sought a transfer to the Pacific theater "to see action against the Japanese." On 5 April 1945 the *PE-56* was dry-docked for maintenance and repairs at Rockland, Maine, including the complete cleaning, inspection, overhaul and pressure testing of her boilers, and servicing of her turbine, all of which were in operational order at the time she returned to service ten days later, on 15 April 1945.

U.S. Navy Yeoman 1st Class, Harold Ralph Rodman, then 21 years of age, had recently returned from Europe, and had been assigned for duty aboard the *PE-56*. With the war against Germany almost at an end, and after surviving the Allied invasions of North Africa, Italy and France, he assured his 16-year-old little sister, Elaine (Mitchell), back in New Jersey, of his perceived safety, telling her, "what could be safer than Portland Harbor?"

On 12 April 1945 President Franklin D. Roosevelt died of a cerebral hemorrhage at Warm Springs in Georgia, and Vice-President Harry S. Truman became President of the United States. By this time the Battle of Okinawa was under way, and Berlin was encircled and under siege by vengeful Soviet forces. Hitler sought final refuge in his Führerbunker behind the Reich Chancellery in Berlin as the imminent surrender of Germany's Third Reich to the Allies was only days away. On 23 April 1945 Hitler's situation had become so critical that he ordered that his former close friend, Reichsmarschall, Hermann Göring, be arrested, after Göring attempted to wrest leadership of the crumbling Reich from the besieged dictator. With the German U-boat pens in France having been captured by the Allies, and despite the futility of further resistance to the Allied onslaught, a fleet of German U-boats had recently departed from their bases in Norway, in a last desperate effort against Allied shipping off the American Northeast coast.

At 8:15 AM on Monday, 23 April 1945 the U.S.S. *Eagle 56* (LCDR, James G. Early, USNR), departed Portland and proceeded out of Portland Harbor to the Casco Bay towing spar training area oboe ("O"), for the purpose of towing a target buoy (the "pickle") for naval aircraft bombing practice exercises. It was a cold, clear day, with moderate seas, unlimited visibility, a few high scattered clouds and a 19 knot wind out of the North-Northwest. At approximately 12:14 PM, while standing by at a dead-stop between exercises, the *PE-56* mysteriously exploded amidships, broke in half and sank at an estimated position of 43 degrees 29 minutes (') 40 seconds (") North Latitude, 70 degrees 06'-45" West Longitude, approximately five miles Southeast of Cape Elizabeth, in waters estimated at 30 to 50 fathoms, or approximately 180 to 300 feet deep.

Immediately after the explosion aboard the *PE-56*, the stern quickly began sinking amidships, though approximately three dozen survivors in the aft crew compartments were able to make their way topside, scramble up the pitching deck to the depth-charge racks, and jump clear before it sank from view in approximately 5 minutes. The severed bow also settled quickly amidships, as her tapered stem rose high in the air, perpendicular to the water, presenting a triangular target with exposed anchors and the large painted numbers "56" visible on the bow. All personnel on the bridge, and almost all those below decks in the bow section, including the CPO (Chief Petty Officer) quarters, radio shack, wardrooms, Officer's quarters, galley, and forward crew compartment, went down with the wreck. Only one man, the Engineering Officer, survived from the sinking bow of the ship, which remained afloat for approximately 12 to 17 minutes, before it, too, went to the bottom.

Machinist's Mate 1st Class, Edward G. Lockhart, later recounted:

> [after the explosion] . . . I traveled into the next compartment . . . the seamen's compartment and mess hall. There I noticed three or four guys lying on the deck and some more of the fellows were going up the ladder into the head and outside to the fantail. I went out on the fantail and I seen the forward part of the ship, and the keel, and it seemed like it was traveling away from the stern. It was floating with about a 20 degree list with the amidships part down. Water was already beginning to run into the aft deck-house and down the ladder. At that point it was sinking pretty rapidly, and the life jackets and life raft went under water . . . I couldn't free it because it was going down too fast. . . . Then most of the fellows were climbing up on the depth-charges and I was the first to go over the side . . . I found a piece of 6 inch by 6 inch (wood timber shoring) about three feet long. The water was cold and had a numbing effect on me . . . I saw various members of the crew, some floating with their heads down. Some holding onto different things. I got so numb I didn't have a clear head after that.

According to Machinist's Mate 1st Class, Harold Petersen: "It [the explosion] threw me head-first into one of the lockers, which stunned me but didn't knock me out." Petersen got back on his feet and stumbled below decks through the flooding ship with his friend, the ship's cook Robert Gurnett Coleman. Petersen urged Coleman: "We've got to get out of here before it sinks or it'll suck us right down," to which Coleman responded, "Pete, I can't swim!" Fighting their way topside after trying unsuccessfully to free a trapped shipmate, Fireman 1st Class Leonard "Leo" Surowiec, Petersen and Coleman abandoned the aft section of the sinking ship. "We dove over and I never saw him (Coleman) again," Petersen said. "He never came up."

Machinist's Mate 2nd Class, John L. Breeze, who had just settled down in the aft crew compartment, was working on a crossword puzzle, and was just about to light his pipe full of Sir Walter Raleigh tobacco when the explosion occurred, throwing him up to the overhead (ceiling), literally launching him out of his shoes. After slamming back down to the deck, in a state of shock his first concern was to find his shoes. With the aft of the ship rapidly listing toward amidships, the compartment began flooding with icy sea water, snapping him back to his senses, as his instinct for survival quickly took over. He later recounted that both escape ladders suspended from the overhead in the aft crews' compartment came loose and fell to the deck as the explosion lifted the ship 3 feet out of the water, breaking her keel, and forcing all hands to scramble to a ladder in the forward crews' quarters, to reach topside (the aft crew living quarters were divided into two compartments, with the crews' quarters behind the engine room bulkhead, and the engineers' quarters at the extreme aft). When they stepped through the door from the aft deck-house, the water was already ankle deep, and they had to crawl up the pitching deck to the fantail and depth-charge racks before going over the side.

As a number of the *PE-56* crewmen prepared to jump clear from the fantail of the sinking stern, they saw a black submarine momentarily broach the surface several hundred yards away. The submarine dove and disappeared quickly, as the startled survivors jumped into the numbing 42 degree waters, and frantically swam from the stern to avoid being pulled down with the wreck. John Breeze later recounted:

> I got up on the after deckhouse right behind (Seaman 1st Class) Johnny Luttrell and ahead of Oscar Davis, . . . stepped out of the after deckhouse . . . into about six inches of water. The ship was going down fast, and Davis mentioned to me, he said, "hey, Breeze, look, there's a

sub" . . . it was completely surfaced but it didn't stay there very long . . . [it was] all black.

At the time of her sinking, the hull and superstructure of the *PE-56* was painted a blue-gray color. Machinist's Mate 3rd Class, Oscar F. Davis stated:

> I was standing under the escape hatch in the aft compartment . . . I heard the explosion and it blew off the ladder I was holding onto. I got out . . . Edwards said there is a submarine over there . . . I saw the sub.

According to Radarman 3rd Class, John A. Wisniewski:

> When I got topside there was a few of the fellows looking around for life jackets and I tried to release the raft on the starboard side. I couldn't get the raft released so I got up on the afterdeck house to see if there were any life jackets there. I saw the submarine on the starboard bow . . . roughly speaking, I would say about 500 yards [away].

When asked if he could have mistaken the severed bow of the *PE-56*, for a submarine, John Wisniewski testified that as he stood on the sinking aft section of the *PE-56*, he could see both the bow of the *PE-56* floating approximately 100 yards away, and the more distant submarine, simultaneously. Gunner's Mate 3rd Class, Lawrence L. Edwards, testified:

> When I got on deck . . . someone shouted get some life jackets, but I saw there wasn't any chances of getting any. The lifeboats were half under water. I looked up the fantail and I saw a man running up there and there wasn't any use in going up there. Then I thought I saw a submarine. . . . At the time I think it was five or six hundred yards. It seemed like a submarine surfaced. It was in a swell and it was sort of lifted.

When asked if the object he saw could have been the bow of the *PE-56*, Lawrence Edwards testified, "I saw the bow of the ship (the *PE-56*), and it was sticking up at the same time." When asked if the explosion could have come from one of the 20 depth-charges stored in the two fantail racks, he testified, "No Sir, I saw them when I came out. They were all right that morning with the safety valves set." Seaman 1st Class, Daniel E. Jaronik, testified:

> Topside I climbed up the fantail and Edwards said, "A submarine," and we looked . . . I looked at it for a couple of seconds . . . It looked all black and I could see red or yellow markings.

When asked if the object he saw could have been the bow of the *PE-56*, Daniel Jaronik testified, "No Sir." And when asked if there were any red or yellow markings on the *PE-56*, Jaronik responded, "No Sir." At the time of the sinking of the *PE-56*, German snorkel fitted U-boats such as the Type IXC/40 "Seewolf" group U-boats were in fact, painted black, and not even the U.S. Navy Office of Naval Intelligence (ONI), had any way of knowing that one particular German U-boat operating in the area of the Gulf of Maine, bore a red and yellow conning tower insignia.

The *PE-56*'s 24 foot whaleboat, located starboard, and her port 21 foot motor dory, both attached to davits amidships, and probably destroyed in the explosion, went down with the wreck of the *PE-56*. The ship also had two life-rafts, also located amidships, fastened to the deck beneath the whaleboat and motor dory, and they were supposed to have automatically released and floated free in the event the ship went down. The life-rafts did not deploy, however, and the few survivors, none of whom were wearing warm clothing, foul-weather gear, or life jackets, struggled in the chilling waters to keep from drowning, clinging to any wreckage that remained afloat, including wood shoring timbers, oil drums, and milk cans which had floated free of the wreck.

As Machinist's Mate Breeze swam to a piece of floating 4 inch by 4 inch wood shoring timber, he came across the lifeless body of Fireman 1st Class, Norris W. Jones, who appeared to have been killed by massive trauma to his back. Though fireman Jones had been working in the boiler (fire) room at the time of the explosion, he appeared to show no signs of burns or scalding injuries. Such injuries would surely have been present had a boiler explosion caused the sinking of the *PE-56*. John Breeze later recounted:

> When I went over the side, within just a few seconds I had to push a fellow named Jonesie's body away . . . he had the twelve to four watch and his body floated toward me . . . the boiler room had to break someplace for his body to come to the surface . . . Not burning or scalding [injuries] but he had a terrible wound in his back. His back had a big hump in it. Probably when the torpedo hit he was thrown against something because it evidently broke his back.

The tremendous explosion was witnessed by Cape Elizabeth's Casco Bay Magnetic Loop Receiving Station (Naval Unit 1-B), at High Head, approximately 5 miles from the *PE-56*, and by the Portland Harbor Entrance Control Post (HECP) at Fort Williams, Portland Head, Maine, approximately 9 miles away. The U.S. Navy destroyer U.S.S. *Selfridge* (DD-357), heading toward the Portland Harbor defenses, in the area of West Cod Ledge, and several other nearby vessels including the destroyer U.S.S. *Woolsey* (DD-437), and the Portland Harbor Light Ship, at that time the U.S.S. *Nantucket* (LV-112), which was armed and acting at the Portland Gate Examination Vessel, witnessed the explosion, sounded General Quarters and proceeded to the scene to conduct rescue operations. Another nearby warship, the U.S. Navy coastal minesweeper U.S.S. *Adamant* (AMc-62), also witnessed the explosion, though she was streaming paravanes as part of her routine, daily mine-clearing operations, so she did not take part in the subsequent rescue operations. The U.S.S. *Selfridge* launched a whaleboat to assist in the rescue of survivors, but it immediately fouled its propeller on floating wreckage, prompting an Officer and several crewmen to dive from the port side of the destroyer to assist in the rescue. Of the 6 Officers and 56 enlisted men (62 total) aboard the *PE-56*, the U.S.S. *Selfridge* was able to rescue only one Officer and nine enlisted men from the frigid waters. Lifeboats from the Portland Harbor Lightship/ Portland Gate Examination Vessel (*LV-112*), recovered the body of Machinist's Mate 2nd Class George W. Neugen, and rescued three additional crewmen, all of whom were suffering from severe shock and exposure (hypothermia).

Earlier that morning the U.S.S. *Selfridge* had been conducting anti-submarine warfare (ASW) exercises approximately 12 miles East of Portland Harbor, on the wreck of the retired U.S. Navy training submarine S-21 (SS-126), which had intentionally been sunk by the Navy on 23 March 1945 in 160 feet of water approximately 3 miles Southeast of Halfway Rock, for use by surface warships as an ASW sonar target. Robert L. Ferree, Helmsman aboard the U.S.S. *Selfridge*, later recounted:

> The *Selfridge* had been out on an anti-submarine training exercise and had a sonar specialist aboard. I was at the helm, and we were returning to port when the explosion was sighted. We came about and headed for the sight at full speed. Approaching, I estimated 35 heads in the water, on our port side. The ship's boat, which was on the starboard side, was lowered and the engine started. Almost immediately a length of line, probably from the sunken ship, was sucked up and fouled the propeller. [It was actually the painter line from the lifeboat itself, which had inadvertently been cast loose out of the boat.] Some time was lost clearing that and some heads disappeared.

Finally, the boat was underway and the crew started picking up people. It was at this time that one or two of our crew dove over the side and swam to the aid of some of the survivors.

According to Lieutenant Commander J.A. Boyd (USN), Commanding Officer aboard the U.S.S. *Selfridge*, "About 15 minutes prior to the explosion, the *PE-56* was tracked briefly at dead in the water," the explosion aboard the *PE-56* resulted in a "white column of smoke and vapor about 100 feet high . . . appeared larger than that from a depth charge, persisted for at least 20 seconds, and had the appearance of an external, rather than an internal underwater explosion." Commander Boyd went on to say "The explosion was very heavy, the ship broke in two immediately. The stern section seemed to be larger than the bow, indicating an explosion forward of amidships." At the time of the explosion aboard the *PE-56*, the U.S.S. *Selfridge* had been steaming in the opposite direction, approximately 7 miles away.

Lieutenant, Guy V. Emro (U.S. Coast Guard), the Commanding Officer aboard the U.S.S. *Nantucket* (*LV-112*), which was only two and a half miles away from the *PE-56* when she exploded, later testified:

> I observed the explosion. It was notable for so much water being in the air . . . The immense amount of water in the air I judged to be about 250 to 300 feet high . . . The explosion must have come from without (outside the ship's hull), due to the immense amount of water and parts of the ship lifted into the air . . . No explosion I have ever seen equaled the force and the amount of water and debris lifted into the air. I have witnessed a boiler blow out--the water tube type of boiler--(the type installed in the *PE-56*) . . . but the explosion could be compared in no way to the power displayed in this one . . . [we] Arrived at the explosion [scene] 24 minutes after [the explosion]. Boats

were put away immediately. Oil, debris and parts of bodies were floating. [We] Picked up survivors, some in motor boat, some in whale boat and one from the ship (*LV-112*) itself. [We] Found that man picked up from side of ship [Machinist's Mate 1st Class, George W. Neugen], when taken aboard was dead. The other survivors were wrapped in blankets, given morphine and liquor. [I] Then requested [a] fast boat from HECP [Harbor Entrance Control Post at Fort Williams, Portland Head], to take survivors to port.

Though Commander Emro had been operating out of Portland and was available to give testimony and to be questioned by the Court of Inquiry, for some unknown reason he was not called as a witness. Only a heavily redacted abstract of the *LV-112*'s deck log was submitted to the Court, and read into evidence. Likewise, the Commander of the *AMc-62* was not called to give testimony, nor was the ship's deck log submitted into evidence. Subsequent Freedom of Information Act (FOIA) records requests to the National Archives, the U.S. Navy and Coast Guard have been unsuccessful in producing copies of the deck logs of either the *LV-112* or the *AMc-62*, regarding the events of 23 April 1945.

According to surviving senior Engineering Officer, Lieutenant (jg) John P. Scagnelli, the only survivor from the forward section of the *PE-56*:

> We were engaged in carrying out exercises which consisted of towing a spar for aerial torpedo bombing practice. we had completed the morning exercises and were standing by awaiting another group of planes. Meanwhile, noon-chow was put down and the men who were not on watch either rested or sat about talking. At approximately 12:14 (PM) the ship was rocked by a terrific explosion which split the ship in half rendering practically everyone unconscious.

Lieutenant Scagnelli, who had just settled down to take a nap when the explosion occurred, was thrown to the bulkhead sustaining an open, horseshoe shaped head wound. He later recounted:

> I was sorta dazed . . . I went into the passageway and the ship (bow) was listing to starboard. The passageway was filled with steam from a broken pipe . . . there was all sorts of debris . . . I went to the CPO quarters where there was a ladder to the main deck. There was a magazine below the ladder and I knew the magazine had not gone off because the ladder wouldn't have been there. The port hatch was partly blocked and I got myself clear and went out past the galley and to open water.

The Commanding Officer of the *PE-56*, Lieutenant James G. Early, who was last seen on the bridge, was killed in the explosion and went down with the bow of the ship. Many of those who survived the explosion, gave way to severe exposure, drowned or were taken down with the wreck. When later asked if he could account for the loss of all of the Officers and crewmen on the bridge and in the chart house, Lieutenant Scagnelli testified:

> Their doors may have been closed and when the explosion occurred that may have slammed them tight. They have two doors, one on the starboard side and one on the aft port side. The port was dogged (locked).

When asked if he felt that most of the men in their living compartments were possibly trapped in the ship's hull after the explosion, Lieutenant Scagnelli testified, "Yes, Sir . . . the explosion rendered a great many of them (the crew) unconscious . . . As I came through I didn't hear any yelling or screaming or calling for help." Many of the *PE-56* Officers and crewmen were thrown against bulkheads and rendered unconscious by the explosion, becoming entrapped below decks, as their only means of escape became flooded, taking many still alive, down to the cold, dark, crushing depths of the North Atlantic, where they suffered agonizing deaths, entombed within the wreckage.

U.S.S. *Selfridge* crewman Edwin Walker, later recounted:

> My station was on the Range Finder, the big eyes on the ship. I was not a very good range finder as the official operator, "Dick" Veit was not on duty that day. I wish I had not been there. When the *PE56* blew up it sounded like a depth charge as I was in the computer room as we had just floated into the Harbor inside the submarine net and General Quarters was over. Immediately GQ was sounded again and I climbed up into the range finder. The range finder was set up for "distance" and immediately the Captain called up for information about the object sticking up out of the water, it actually was the bow of the *PE56* sinking fast. To me it looked like the smoke stack of a merchant ship and I told the Captain such. I could not get a good look at it and he said "Hell, I can see better with my binoculars." . . . During the next several minutes I watched the survivors and the dead. Our ship attempted rescue and our whale boat I think picked up 13 survivors. Of those one was put in the torpedo shack as a substitute sick bay. They wrapped him (Seaman 2nd Class, Paul J. Knapp) in blankets and he said he was OK, but he collapsed and died. I think 12 men were saved. I looked down into the cold clear water and watched several clinging to floating junk and such but the water was so cold they soon turned loose and slowly sank. I always wish I had not been there and saw this . . . Watching the crew of the *PE56* slowly loose grip and slowly sink was difficult. The *Selfridge* was a duck in the water, sitting as a perfect target for a submarine and we anticipated a torpedo coming.

Our opinion was "sub." I hate to remember one sailor in a white T shirt, husky, strong like a wrestler holding onto a floating barrel or something like that and he had his arms around it, slowly he relaxed and slipped under the water. Vivid memory, I watched him sink. He let out his breath and bubbles rose to the surface but he held my attention until he was no longer visible. My thoughts were "there goes some mother's beloved son and she will never know how he died." I wished I knew who he was so that I could have told her.

After taking aboard ten survivors, at 12:48 PM the U.S.S. *Selfridge* made a sound contact on her sonar indicating the presence of a potential enemy submarine at an estimated range of 1,125 yards to the Northeast. Helmsman, Robert Ferree, later recounted:

> When the sonar man called out the contact the Captain immediately got under way and ordered the depth-charge attack. Many of the *Selfridge* crewmen watched in horror as the destroyer's screws began to turn, sucking several of the *PE-56*'s exhausted survivors who were so close to rescue, to their deaths. The sonar specialist on board gave his opinion that the contact was a good one. The Commodore (Frank Walker, USN), objected to leaving survivors, if any, in the water, but Captain Boyd had no choice.

The U.S.S. *Selfridge* closed on the contact and at approximately 12:53 PM, dropped a 9 depth-charge (Mk IX Mod. 2) pattern set to explode at 50, 100 and 150 foot depths, all of which detonated, without positive results. Before making a second pass over the target the *Selfridge* was ordered by HECP to break off the attack, to pick up the survivors rescued and bodies recovered by her whaleboat and the Portland Gate Examination Vessel (total of 13 survivors rescued and 2 bodies recovered), to retrieve her whaleboat, and to proceed to Portland to transfer the survivors to the U.S. Naval Dispensary at Grand Trunk Pier, where many received plasma, morphine and "medicinal whiskey." *Selfridge* crewman Edwin Walker recounted:

> After picking up survivors, our ship rushed to dock . . . where the survivors were taken off to hospitals. I looked down into the faces of the survivors as they were carried off in stretchers, shocked, wounded, just hardly alive, frozen, miserable.

Only the bodies of two dead crewmen, MM1c, George W. Neugen, and S2c, Paul J. Knapp, were recovered from the expansive wreckage-strewn oil slick. Five Officers and 42, enlisted men including all but one Officer (Lt. John Scagnelli) in the bow section at the time of the explosion, were killed and went down to the bottom with the wreckage of the *PE-56* (see Appendix I).

Subsequent U.S. Navy assessment of the of the U.S.S. *Selfridge*'s sonar contact and depth-charge attack on the suspect target, determined the anomaly was likely a "non-sub contact," possibly a naturally occurring bottom structure such as a "rock pinnacle" or part of the wreck of the *PE-56* itself. An extensive side-scan sonar survey of the area of the depth-charge attack, conducted in July of 2000, however, revealed no such geological bottom features in that particular area, nor any part of the wreckage of the *PE-56*.

The loss of 49 Officers and crewmen aboard the *PE-56* was among the greatest U.S. Naval tragedies within American coastal waters, and was the worst U.S. Naval loss in New England waters during the war. Coincidentally, the *PE-56*, which had rescued the survivors of the U.S.S. *Jacob Jones II*, the first U.S. warship to be sunk within American coastal waters by a German U-boat during World War II, ultimately became the last such victim.

Within hours of the sinking of the *PE-56*, the waters off Cape Elizabeth and Casco Bay were being swept by a fleet of U.S. Naval vessels including the (ComDesRon 13) destroyers U.S.S. *Selfridge*, U.S.S. *Craven* (*DD-382*), U.S.S. *Woolsey* (*DD-437*), U.S.S. *Earle* (*DD-635*), the destroyer escort U.S.S. *Evarts* (*DE-5*) and the Coast Guard manned patrol frigate U.S.S. *Brunswick* (*PF-68*), assisted by the U.S.S. *Eberle* (*DD-430*), U.S.S. *Muskegon* (*PF-24*), U.S.S. *Rinehart* (*DE-196*), U.S.S. *Uniontown* (*PF-65*) and U.S.S. *Wingfield* (*DE-194*) comprising Task Group 60.3, conducting anti-submarine warfare operations well into the late evening. Also joining in the search for the suspect German U-boat were three U.S. Navy Consolidated PBY "Catalina" flying-boats, and two twin-engine Lockheed Vega-37 "Ventura" PV-1 patrol-bomber aircraft from the Brunswick Naval Air Station. By this time, however, the U-boat had already crept off into the relative safety of deeper waters, submerged on her electric motors and concealed by the areas rough bottom topography, far from shore.

On Tuesday 24 April 1945, the U.S.S. *Muskegon* (Lt. Joe L. Horne, USCG), assisted by U.S.S. *Earle*, U.S.S. *Eberle*, U.S.S. *Uniontown* and the U.S. Coast Guard cutter #92004 (Robert E. Dennison, , USCG), of Task Group 60.3, were conducting an anti-submarine patrol, hunting the U-boat off Monhegan Island, Maine, approximately 50 miles East Northeast of Portland. At 7:00 AM the USCGC-92004 was monitoring sound contacts from a nearby fishing boat, and a large freighter "making good interference" streaming a "Foxer" mechanical sound-maker, a countermeasure designed to distract and divert German Type V (T-5) acoustic-homing torpedoes. At 7:30 AM the 92004 reported: "110 degrees magnetic, very likely submarine contact. Watch reports sub blew tanks." The search for the U-boat began, as one of the destroyer escorts began generating smoke to obscure visual detection of the hunting warships. The search continued into the early afternoon, and at 3:12 PM the *Muskegon* reported:

> Sighted smoke on surface from no visible source bearing 013 degrees true, distance 3 miles. All hands

to General Quarters. Smoke resembled diesel exhaust and was very near Roaring Bull Rock Buoy apparently moving upwind, presumed to be enemy submarine using schnorchel . . . proceeding to investigate.

By 3:17 PM the *Muskegon* reported: "smoke disappeared suddenly." At 4:42 the *Muskegon* acquired a contact on her QJA Type sonar in 20 fathoms at Lat. 43 degrees 52'-54" North/Long. 69 degrees 11'-48" West, and at 11.5 knots she fired 8 Mark IX depth-charges from her K-guns, set to detonate at 50 feet. All charges detonated with negative results. The *Muskegon* was ordered to barrier patrol between Burnt Island and Roaring Bull Rock, as *Earle* and *Uniontown* made successive runs over the area without regaining contact. By 7:48 PM the ships reformed a scouting line abeam at 2,000 yard intervals "carrying out retiring search for enemy submarine."

The search continued that evening and into the early hours of the morning of Wednesday 25 April 1945, when at 3:50 AM the 92004 reported: "Sub contact. Can hear electric engines and blow of tanks. Relative bearing 328 degrees." Possibly the 92004 had detected the U-boat attempting to surface and ventilate. The contact was lost, but the search continued until 12:34 PM when the *Muskegon* reported: "detached to investigate sonar contact which gave good record traces." and at 12:50 PM the contact in 72 fathoms (approximately 430 feet), at the mouth of Penobscot Bay was "classified as possible bottomed submarine" with "strong echoes." At 12:51 the *Muskegon* fired a full pattern of Mark X (Mk 10) "Hedgehog" projectiles with negative results at Lat. 43 degrees 30' North/Long. 69 degrees 42' West. Hedgehogs were a bow-mounted battery of 24, 7.2-inch "ahead-throwing" 65 pound spigot launched, contact-fused depth-bombs, each containing a 35 pound Torpex shaped-charge warhead, fired in a circular or elliptical pattern up to 270 yards ahead of the attacking warship, and detonated on contact. At 1:01 PM the *Muskegon* regained contact and at 1:07 she fired another full pattern of Hedgehogs approximately 200 yards from the first attack, in 68 fathoms, with no detonations. At 1:37 she again regained contact, maneuvered to re-attack and at 1:51 fired a third full pattern of Hedgehogs with a single explosion after 29 seconds, believed to have been the "entire pattern striking bottom." At that time the *Muskegon* blew a gasket on her 4-inch auxiliary steam line to the galley, in her number one fire-room and at 1:53 PM she discontinued the search to clear the area and effect repairs. The *Earle* and *Eberle* maneuvered in the area and made several subsequent depth-charge attacks, before the *Muskegon* completed repairs at 3:05 PM and resumed independent search in the vicinity. The warships formed a scouting line abeam at 2,500 yard intervals at 4:08 PM and swept the area several times without regaining any good sonar contacts. The ZNP type U.S. Navy blimp *K-38* was dispatched to the area of the sound contacts and subsequent attacks, but her magnetic (airborne) anomaly detection (MAD) gear was not functioning properly, and unable to acquire a contact, she soon returned to her base, the Naval Air Station at South Weymouth, Massachusetts.

On Thursday, 26 April 1945 William Heckendorf was a combat air-crewman aboard a PBY-5A amphibious "Catalina" flying boat from patrol squadron VPB-92 out of the Quonset Point (Rhode Island) Naval Air Station, flying anti-submarine patrol cover in the Gulf of Maine. The patrol squadron had been placed on alert and notified of the presence of several German U-boats believed to be operating in the area. According to William Heckendorf:

> At approximately 3:00 PM we picked up a blip on our radar that there was a submarine sitting on top of the water about 40 miles away charging their batteries so we honed [sic] in on it and saw the oil slick on the water where it had been sitting. We dropped our sonar gear and picked up the sound of a submarine's engine. We pinpointed the sub and dropped two 500lb depth charges.

About 5 minutes later the ocean was full of debris and oil.
I took a picture with the navy K25 camera but there were
no survivors.

It is possible the U-boat that was attacked by the Catalina was
the one that torpedoed and sank the *PE-56*, and it was a common
ploy for U-boat Commanders to discharge oil and to fire debris out of
their torpedo tubes in order to confuse their attackers into believing
they had destroyed their prey, ending the attack.

On 29 April 1945 a U.S. Navy Grumman "F6F" Hellcat fighter-
plane on a training flight from Charlestown, Rhode Island, sighted a
submarine briefly surfaced approximately 10 miles East of Wellfleet,
Cape Cod, and a number of U.S. Navy and Coast Guard warships,
the U.S.S. *Eberle*, U.S.S. *Evarts*, U.S.S. *Gleaves* (*DD-423*), U.S.S. *Dale
W. Peterson* (*DE-337*), U.S.S. *Sturtevant* (*DE-239*), USCGC *Dione*,
USCGC *92004*, *SC-1022*, *SC-1301*, and *YMS-74*, were dispatched to
the scene to search for the sub. This was likely the same U-boat that
torpedoed and sank the *PE-56*, now heading South after departing
the Gulf of Maine.

Within a week of the sinking of the *PE-56*, the survivors were
interviewed by the press, and the U.S. Navy convened a Court of
Inquiry presided over by Captain Ernest J. Freeman (USNR), who
also happened to be the Commanding Officer (CO) of the Portland
Naval Station, and therefore ultimately accountable for the loss of
the *PE-56* and her crew. The Court of Inquiry was convened for the
purpose of investigating the circumstances surrounding the sinking
of the *PE-56*, to interview survivors and witnesses, to make Findings
on the cause of her loss, and to issue Recommendations. Other
members of the Court of Inquiry included Lieutenant Commander,
William H. Coolidge (USNR), and Lieutenant Commander, Jackson
B. Heirs, (USNR), with Lieutenant Commander, Norman Kaufman
(USNR), acting as the Judge Advocate. The Court of Inquiry was
not conducted in the traditional manner in which witnesses were

examined in a courtroom before the standard tribunal. The survivors of the *PE-56* were first admonished that "there was no submarine, and you did not see any submarine" before being informally questioned while still in the Grand Trunk Naval Dispensary, by a young U.S. Navy Lieutenant, while 21-year-old Naval Reserve member of the WAVES (Women Accepted for Volunteer Emergency Service), Legal Yeoman and stenographer, Mary Alice Heyd, took shorthand notes of their testimony. Mary Alice (Heyd) Hultgren later recounted how she was convinced by the survivors' testimony that they had been the victims of a U-boat torpedo attack.

According to testimony given by Lieutenant (jg) Scagnelli:

> All engines and boilers were in good condition and recently had been overhauled . . . during her last complete overhaul . . . in December 1944 . . . they (the boilers) were given a hydrostatic test . . . to a maximum pressure of three hundred and twenty five (325 psi) pounds.
>
> During her most recent overhaul (5 April 1945 to 15 April, 1945), "the [water] tubes [and drums] were all wire brushed and internally cleaned," after which she underwent a "visual inspection of all pressure parts . . . [which] consisted of a steaming test. The test disclosed that the boilers were in good operation condition and there was no evidence of any weakness or steam leaks . . . there was no sign of any weakness in the riveted joints or caustic embrittlement (evidence of metal fatigue) in her boilers. Watertender, Joseph C. Priestas, later recounted, there was "no explosion of the boilers. Fifteen minutes before the explosion the boilers were all right."

Machinist's Mate 2nd Class, Harold H. Petersen, later recounted:

> I am positive . . . there is no 250 psi [boiler] that is

going to do the damage to a ship that that did . . . from forward to stern. It was a huge explosion . . . in fact, at first I thought, maybe we hit a mine or something . . . a boiler can't do that much damage.

When asked what the explosion sounded like, he said, "It sounded like a dynamite boom . . . it was big . . . it lifted us right up." According to Machinist's Mate 2nd Class, John Breeze, at the time the *PE-56* exploded she had been at a dead stop, standing-by, but still making steam, with a pair of 12 horsepower motors driving two loud air-compressors (blowers) stoking the fire boxes by forced-draft in the pressurized fire (boiler) room. These blowers were the "noisiest" part of the ship at the time of the explosion, and were located near amidships, at the bulkhead aft of the boiler room (near structural frame # 56), in the general area of the detonation.

Several of the survivors also testified that they observed dead fish in the water after the explosion and sinking of the *PE-56*, indicative of the effects of an external underwater explosion, such as that caused by the detonation of a mine, depth-charge, or torpedo. Machinist's Mate 1st Class, Edward G. Lockhart, testified: "[I observed] quite a few large ones. Seven or eight or more than that. . . . " When asked what he had observed after the sinking, Machinist's Mate 2nd Class, Harold Petersen, testified "Yes, Sir, dead fish. When we came topside the water was pretty muddy."

Also conspicuously absent from the Court of Inquiry proceedings were the deck Officers and sonarmen of the U.S.S. *Selfridge*, which had steamed from Portland to Norfolk, Virginia, several hours after the sinking of the *PE-56*, where she operated as flagship for Allied warships escorting a merchant convoy to Oran, Algeria (North Africa).

Despite the eyewitness testimony from survivors regarding the surfaced submarine, the subsequent depth-charge attacks on sonar contacts, and evidence of the ship's recent maintenance, the Court of Inquiry concluded "the cause of the [accident] was the result of a boiler explosion, the cause of which could not be determined."

> It is the opinion of the Judge Advocate General that the deaths of MM1c Neugen and S2c Knapp (the two bodies recovered), . . . and injuries to U.S. Naval personnel, listed as injured as a result of the subject disaster, occurred on 23 April 1945, not as the result of their own misconduct . . . those (47) listed therein as missing died on April 23, 1945, by reason of drowning and that each died in line of duty, and not due to his own misconduct . . . not the result of enemy action.

Curiously, though the U.S. Navy had allegedly determined that a catastrophic boiler failure (mechanical malfunction), caused the loss of an American warship, resulting in great loss of life, the Court of Inquiry made none of the customary "Recommendations." Apparently the Navy was not genuinely convinced of the boiler explosion theory, as it neglected to issue any Bureau of Ships (BuShips) advisories regarding the inspection, servicing, repair or replacement of the Navy's many Thornycroft Bureau Express type water-tube boilers, which were installed in a number of other small surface combatants in active service at that time.

According to the destroyer U.S.S. *Craven's* (*DD-382*) war diary, "Eagle boat exploded and sank in area today. Cause undetermined, may have been enemy submarine." According to the U.S. Navy's Bureau of Ships (BuShips): Construction and Repair, Statistics Division, regarding the cause of the loss of the *PE-56*, "Exact nature of cause of explosion is undetermined. Might have been an enemy mine or torpedo." Nowhere on the BuShips U.S.S. *Eagle 56* Information Sheet do the words "boiler explosion" appear. The U.S. Navy Eastern Sea Frontier War Diary: Activity Prior 24 April 1945 (RE: EAD 1215/23) COMINCH (U.S. Navy Commander-in-Chief) evaluation, states: "PE 56 exploded and sunk from unknown cause possibly by U-boat."

A formerly classified letter from Rear Admiral, Felix Gygax, Commandant of the First Naval District and Boston Navy Yard, dated 1 June 1945, contained the following comments regarding the Court of Inquiry findings:

> 1. The Convening Authority has determined by separate investigation that so far as is known there were no friendly mines, torpedoes, depth-charges or other explosive mechanisms that were unaccounted for and that could have caused the explosion that resulted in the loss of the U.S.S. *Eagle (PE-56)*;
>
> 2. With respect to that part of the opinion of the court of inquiry giving the cause of the accident as that of a boiler explosion, the Convening Authority considers that the evidence does not support this unqualified conclusion and believes that there is at least equal evidence to support the conclusion that the explosion was that of a device outside the ship, the exact nature of which is undetermined. It might have been an enemy mine or an enemy torpedo;
>
> 3. It would seem that the boiler explosion, if it occurred, and in any case, the disrupted steam connections, would have been incident to, and could have augmented the effect of, a water column produced by an explosion outside the vessel;
>
> 4. Subject to the foregoing remarks, the proceedings, findings, opinion and recommendation of the court of inquiry in the attached case are approved."

Though clearly influenced by the overwhelming weight of evidence supporting the theory of an external underwater explosion consistent with an enemy torpedo, based upon these rather equivocal recommendations of the Convening Authority, Rear Admiral Felix

Gygax, the Court of Inquiry findings were changed from "possible boiler explosion," to "cause undetermined." In either case the Navy's findings resulted in the determination "not enemy action," depriving the 49 brave young Officers and crewmen killed aboard the *PE-56* posthumous recognition (as well as those wounded survivors), for their sacrifice, in the form of Purple Heart Medals.

The maximum operating pressure of the *PE-56's* two small Bureau Express type oil-fired boilers was only 250 pounds per square inch (psi), and each contained a maximum of only 750 gallons of water. These were not high-pressure boilers with operating pressures of 1,000+ psi, and were hardly sufficient to generate such a violent explosion, and tremendous 100 to 300 foot vertical water column as described by the survivors and witnesses aboard nearby vessels. A number of the world's foremost authorities in ship construction have evaluated the evidence surrounding the sinking of the *PE-56*, and have concluded that the dynamics of the explosion and witness accounts point to an external underwater explosion consistent with a mine or torpedo detonation. The mine possibility has been excluded since the incident occurred approximately 9 miles Southeast of the Portland Harbor defenses and minefields, the waters in the area were regularly swept for mines, none of which were ever located, and no U-boat mining operations had been conducted in Gulf of Maine waters for more than two years prior to that event.

Marine/naval architect and forensic engineer, William Garzke, of Gibbs & Cox, who has written extensively about the sinkings of the R.M.S. *Titanic* and the D.K.M. *Bismarck*, has determined the torpedo theory to be the most plausible explanation for the sinking of the *PE-56*, and that the boiler explosion theory was extremely unlikely.

Based upon the engineering plans and technical specifications of the Eagle Class's low pressure boilers, Mr. Garzke concurred with Admiral Gygax's assessment. He believes that the boilers may have been compromised, but only secondary to a tremendous external, underwater explosion that broke the ship apart. Failure of the ship's boilers alone might have blown off her boiler room ventilators, but would not have generated sufficient force to have torn the ship apart. Though not a single other Eagle Boat sub-chaser of her class, 60 of which were constructed, was ever lost due to a catastrophic boiler failure, at least one German U-boat had reached the Gulf of Maine and is known to have been operating in the area when the *PE-56* exploded and sank.

At the time of the sinking of the *PE-56* the entire North Atlantic was an active war zone, with the American Northeast coast heavily patrolled by German U-boats. On 5 April 1945 the German Type IXC/40 U-boat *U-857* under command of Kapitanleutnant, Rudolph Premauer, torpedoed the 8,537 ton Atlantic Refining Company tanker S.S. *Atlantic States*, in the Gulf of Maine. She was located on sonar by destroyer escorts U.S.S. *Gustafson* and U.S.S. *Micka*, approximately 22 miles Northeast of Provincetown, Massachusetts, on 7 April 1945, attacked with Mk10 Hedgehogs, and was recorded as having been sunk with all 59 Officers and crewmen aboard, at an estimated position of 42 degrees 22' North; 69 degrees 46' West. During this period the Type IXC/40 U-boats *U-190*, *U-548*, and *U-879* were patrolling the areas South of Nova Scotia, Canada, and on 16 April 1945, in an attack virtually identical to that executed against the *PE-56* one week later, the *U-190* under Oberleutnant zur See, Hans-Edwin Reith, torpedoed and sank the 590 ton Canadian minesweeper H.M.C.S. *Esquimalt* off Halifax, Nova Scotia, with the loss of all but 26 of her 70 Officers and crewmen, before surrendering at Bay of Bulls, Newfoundland, on 11 May 1945. On 14 April 1945, *U-548*, under command of Oberleutnant zur See, Erich Krempl, is believed to have torpedoed and sank the 6,959 ton freighter S.S. *Belgian Airman*, and while later attacking a convoy to the North, was located by destroyer escorts U.S.S. *Buckley* (*DE-51*) and U.S.S. *Reuben James II* (*DE-153*) of the American Bogue Class escort-carrier U.S.S. *Card* (*CVE-11*) hunter/killer Task Group 22.10, and sunk by Hedgehog attack with all 59 Officers and crewmen aboard lost on 19

April 1945 at 42 degrees 19' North Lat./61 degrees 45' West Long., approximately 150 miles South Southeast of Halifax, Nova Scotia.

On the morning of 30 April 1945, *U-879* under command of Kapitanleutnant, Erwin Manchen, was located East of Norfolk, Virginia, while attacking convoy KN382, came under depth-charge and Hedgehog attack by patrol frigate U.S.S. *Nachez* (*PF-2*) and destroyer escorts U.S.S. *Coffman* (*DE-191*), U.S.S. *Bostwick* (*DE-103*) and U.S.S. *Thomas* (*DE-102*), and was sunk at 36 degrees 34' North Lat./74 degrees West Long., with the loss of all 52 Officers and crewmen aboard.

During April and early May of 1945 the U.S. Navy and Army Air Forces were placed on a high state of alert, mobilizing an aggressive anti-submarine campaign code named "Operation Teardrop" (initially "Bumblebee"). That massive force of sea-power was comprised of four escort carriers and more than forty destroyers and destroyer escorts, formed in two successive barriers. This was in response to the perceived, though false threat that this latest fleet of German U-boats headed to the American Northeast coast could be towing submersible launch containers from which V-2 (A-4) type guided rockets; or deck mounted containers from which Fieseler Fi-103 (V-1) pulse-jet powered cruise type missiles, or so-called "robot-bombs," would be launched against New York City. According to Thomas Houston, S3C formerly aboard the *PT-314* stationed at the Motor Torpedo Boat base (Ron 4) at Melville, Rhode Island:

> In the last few weeks before Germany's surrender we were on constant alert, ready to be sent out to hunt U-boats that were known to be operating in our waters. We were under strict orders not to talk to anyone about the German U-boats known to be operating off the New England coast, so as not to create panic among the public.

On 23 April 1945, one German U-boat in particular, *U-853* had recently arrived at her patrol station in or about Kriegsmarine grid-area (Marinequadrat) "*BA-94*" in the Gulf of Maine, and was operating in the area of Cape Elizabeth and Casco Bay at the time the *PE-56* exploded and sank. The *U-853*, nicknamed "Der Seiltaenzer" or "The Tightrope Walker" by her crew, was a 252 foot long, 1,144 ton (1,257 tons submerged) steel hull, diesel/electric powered, "schnorchel" (snorkel) equipped, Type IXC/40 German U-boat, constructed by Deschimag-AG Weser in Bremen, Germany where her keel was laid on 21 August 1942, she was launched on 11 March 1943 and commissioned on 25 June 1943. The *U-853* was armed with four bow and two stern (533mm) 21-inch torpedo tubes for which she could carry up to 22 torpedoes, and mounted one 37mm "flak" (fleigerabwehrkanone) anti-aircraft gun on the aft deck and two twin 20mm Mauser flak guns on the "wintergarten" (winter garden), the raised gun platform aft of the conning tower. She was powered by either her twin 2,200 horsepower MAN (Maschinenfabrik Augsburg-Nurnberg AG), manufactured 9-cylinder, 4-stroke M9V 40/46 supercharged compression-ignition diesel engines, or her two 500 horsepower Siemens-Schuckert 2GU 345/34 electric motors, and was capable of speeds of 18.3 knots surfaced, or 7.3 knots submerged, with a maximum range on her diesels of 11,400 nautical miles.

On 25 May 1944 while conducting weather reporting duties in the North Atlantic, the surfaced *U-853* sighted the distant silhouette of a massive, fast moving ocean liner that turned out to be the British flagged troop-transport R.M.S. *Queen Mary*, carrying nearly 14,000 U.S. Army soldiers destined to take part in the 6 June 1944 Invasion of Normandy. The unescorted, though zigzagging 80,000 ton *Queen Mary* was steaming at more than 28 knots, too fast for the *U-853* to get into attack position. Soon after that encounter the *U-853* came under attack by three rocket-firing British "Swordfish" aircraft from the merchant aircraft catapult (MAC) ships S.S. *Ancylus* (British flagged, Anglo-Saxon Petroleum Co. Ltd., 483 foot, 12,190 ton tanker), and S.S. *MacKendrick*, but after ordering the *U-853*'s flak crew into action, her Commanding Officer, Kapitanleutnant Helmut

Sommer ordered her to crash dive to safety.

Later on that same patrol, on 17 June 1944 the surfaced *U-853* came under strafing attack by two U.S. Navy Grumman F4F "Wildcat" fighter planes from the escort-carrier U.S.S. *Croatan* (*CVE-25*), after being located by high-frequency direction-finding (H/F-D/F or "Huff-Duff") detection equipment, while making a weather reporting radio transmission. Kapitanleutnant, Helmut Sommer, was badly injured on the bridge by .50-caliber machine gun bullet fragments, with 2 crewmen Bootsmaat: Petty Officer 3rd Class or Coxswain, Kurt Schweichler 26.08.15 and Maschinengefreiter or Machinist's Mate 3rd Class, Karl-Heinz Loffler 07.05.25), killed and 12 wounded. The *U-853* dove to evade her attackers and returned to base at Lorient, France, for repairs, before transiting to another U-boat base at Flensburg, Germany, under temporary command of Korvettenkapitan Gunter Kuhnke (between 24 August and 15 October 1944), where she was fitted with a snorkel. The *U-853* transferred to Kiel, Germany, on 6 February 1945 before sailing for Horten, then Stavanger, Norway, where she arrived on 14 February 1945. First Watch Officer (IWO), Oberleutnant zur See (Lieutenant, senior grade), Helmut Frömsdorf, 23 years of age, had recently assumed command of the boat, and on 23 February 1945 she departed Stavanger on her second and final patrol, headed for the New England coast with 55 Officers and crewmen aboard.

Born in Schimmelwitz-Silesia, Germany on 26 March 1921, Helmut Frömsdorf entered as a cadet in the Seaman Branch of the Kriegsmarine (German Navy), with Class XII/1939, he completed Officer training in November of 1941 and served with the 1st and 22nd U-Flotillas, before being promoted to Oberleutnant zur See, on 1 December 1943. On 26 March 1945 while crossing the North Atlantic, Commander Frömsdorf celebrated his 24th birthday. Commander Frömsdorf was operating under orders to seek out and attack Allied shipping in her designated patrol area, the coastal waters between Halifax, Nova Scotia and New York.

Apparently, former Commander Sommer was concerned for the safety of his Officers and crew under young Lieutenant Commander Frömsdorf. Sommer's wife later wrote that her husband thought Frömsdorf was:

> very young and ambitious when he became commander. My husband asked him again and again not to act frivolously, for he knew the end of the war was near and . . . that all the fine fellows of the crew should survive.

Apparently, a number of the *U-853*'s Officers and crewmen were unhappy when Frömsdorf took command of their boat. Before the *U-853* departed Norway on her last patrol, 20-year-old Maschinenobergefreiter (Machinest's Mate 2nd Class) Freidrich Volk, told his mother that he feared the mission because he had no faith in Frömsdorf. Theodore Womer, a *U-853* crewman who had missed the last cruise because of illness, later wrote that "He [Frömsdorf] was a different personality [than Sommer] . . . At least some of the crew believed Frömsdorf was out to get a decoration." Frömsdorf's sister Helga Deisting of Rothenburg, Germany recalled his last letter to their parents:

> I am lucky in these difficult days of my fatherland to have the honor of commanding this submarine, and it is my duty to accept . . . I'm not very good at last words, so goodbye for now and give my sister my love.

Bearing the weathered and deteriorating conning tower insignia illustrating a red trotting horse on a yellow shield, on 23 April 1945, while patrolling off the shipping approaches to Portland, Maine, the submerged *U-853*, under power of her electric motors and masked by the noisy wake of the U.S.S. *Selfridge*, silently closed on the stationary *PE-56*, and at a range of approximately 500 to 600 yards, destroyed the aged sub-chaser like a sitting duck, with either a single Type V (T-5) passive-acoustic homing torpedo, or a

"Facherschuss" fan launch or simultaneous spread of two or more unguided Type G7e (T-2) torpedoes (see Appendix II). One such torpedo passed beneath the shallow 8.5 foot draft keel of the *PE-56*, and the magnetic proximity fuse detonated the warhead under her starboard side amidships, near the area of the loud air-compressors, lifting the ship out of the water, breaking her keel and tearing her in half. The *U-853* momentarily broached the surface after the *PE-56* exploded, possibly due to her failure to maintain proper trim control upon launch of her torpedo(es), (see Appendix III). The *U-853* avoided serious damage during the hasty depth-charge attack conducted by the U.S.S. *Selfridge*, and took advantage of the areas rough bottom topography of underwater hills and canyons, to avoid subsequent detection as she made a silent retreat to deeper waters. For the next week and a half the *U-853* continued her patrol along the New England coast, slowly working her way South, past Massachusetts Bay and Cape Cod, and into Rhode Island Sound.

Cryptanalysts at the top-secret U.S. Navy COMINCH (Commander in Chief, U.S. Fleet) "Ultra" decryption center and Submarine-Tracking Room known as "Op20G" (Op-20-G), in Washington, DC, and Britain's Naval (decrypt) Section at Bletchley Park (Station X) in Buckinghamshire, Northwest of London, were constantly monitoring German encrypted radio transmissions employing the newest four-rotor "Enigma" code called "Triton" ('Shark" to the British). Exercising strict orders of radio silence, transmissions from this last group of U-boats were primarily brief weather reports to BdU (Befehlshaber der Unterseeboote) Commander in Chief, U-boats. The transmissions from *U-853* employed the new "Kurier" (Courier) burst-transmitter, which reduced the time of transmission (Kurzsignal) "short-signal" to mere seconds, decreasing the chance of detection (known as acquiring a "cut," two or more of which could be used to triangulate a fixed position) by Allied Huff-Duff equipment. During the final weeks of her patrol, Op20G tracked the *U-853* as she made her way into the

Gulf of Maine and down along Casco Bay, in Marinequadrat "Bruno Anton-Neun Vier" (marine grid-square BA-94), before traveling South past Cape Cod. Recently declassified records clearly show that U.S. Naval Intelligence knew of the presence of the *U-853* (Contact 250153Z) in the area at the time of the sinking of the *PE-56*, then tracked it as it traveled to the South toward Cape Cod. U.S. Navy F20-Teletype COMINCH dispatch 251515 to the Commander of the Eastern Sea Frontier on 25 April 1945 recently declassified by the National Security Agency (NSA) stated "one (U-boat) possibly 3600 6930 moving West to SW from radar contact 250153Z alternatively Gulf of Maine from PE incident." Subsequent secret COMINCH dispatch 281511 of 28 April 1945 added "one (U-boat) possibly . . . in Gulf of Maine from attack 271438Z (PE incident)." At some point, probably after 27 April 1945 the *U-853* departed the Gulf of Maine and slowly headed South past Cape Cod and into Rhode Island Sound. For security reasons, however, this highly classified information regarding the presence of the *U-853* in the area of the sinking of the *PE-56*, was not shared by the Office of Naval Intelligence (ONI), with the Court of Inquiry, investigating the loss of the *PE-56*.

Though there is no evidence the *U-853* transmitted any message to BdU regarding the sinking of the *PE-56*, this was not unusual, as "Boebachtungsdienst" (B-Dienst) the German radio monitoring and cryptographic service had growing suspicions that their own encrypted transmissions might be compromised and used to triangulate a fix on the transmitting U-boat, hence the strict orders of radio discipline and the development of countermeasures such as Kurier. Information regarding the sinking of the *PE-56* would certainly have been recorded in the *U-853*'s "Kriegstagebuch" (KTB) War Diary, but that was ultimately lost with the U-boat. Similarly, there is no record of the *U-190* (OLzS Reith) ever notifying BdU of her sinking of the Bangor Class minesweeper H.M.C.S. *Esquimalt* off Halifax on 16 April 1945. Strict radio discipline exercised by U-boats by this stage in the war has also led to considerable post-war debate over the exact identity of the particular U-boats that torpedoed the S.S. *Atlantic States* (5 April 45), and S.S. *Belgian Airman* (14 April 45), and about the precise areas or operation of *U-548* (OlzS Kremple), *U-857* (KL Premauer) and *U-879* (KL Manchen), before their respective losses.

On 29 April 1945 Adolf Hitler married Eva Braun in a private ceremony in his Berlin bunker, and he appointed Kriegsmarine Grossadmiral, Karl Dönitz, as his successor as the second, and last Fuehrer of Germany's Third Reich. On 30 April 1945 Hitler and his bride committed suicide, and Dönitz assumed leadership of the Third Reich. On 4 May 1945 at 3:14 PM (EST), the German High Command transmitted a radio dispatch from BdU and Grossadmiral Dönitz, ordering: "All U-boats, attention all U-boats, cease fire at once, stop all hostile action against Allied shipping, Dönitz." It will never be known if Commander Frömsdorf failed to receive this dispatch, possibly due to radio equipment malfunction, or whether he did receive the message, and foolishly chose to disregard it. It is possible the *U-853*'s radio equipment had been damaged by any one of the many depth-charge or Hedgehog attacks conducted by the U.S.S. *Selfridge*, U.S.S. *Muskegon*, U.S.S. *Evarts* or the U.S.S. *Eberle*, as the Allies lost contact with the *U-853* before she departed the Gulf of Maine.

On the morning of Saturday, May 5, 1945, Ensign John Gordon "Brad" Bradley, was piloting his Grumman TBM "Avenger" torpedo bomber off Montauk Point, the East tip of Long Island, New York, along with his Radioman 3rd Class Clifford Brinson, on a routine anti-submarine training mission. Bradley and Brinson were members of the U.S. Navy's composite squadron VC-15 out of Fentress Field (now known as Naval Auxiliary Landing Field Fentress) in Chesapeake, Virginia, but were assigned to Seaplane Hangar 3 at the Quonset Naval Air Station (NAS) in North Kingstown, Rhode Island, where they were taking part in ASD AF (Anti-Submarine Development Atlantic Fleet) exercises with U.S. Navy subs out of Submarine Base

New London in Groton, Connecticut. Their area of operations was between Fisher's Island, New York, and Westerly, Rhode Island. At approximately 10:30 AM, Bradley spotted a surfaced submarine through the fog and clouds, heading Easterly in the direction of Block Island's Southwest Ledge (the distance between Long Island, New York, and Block Island, Rhode Island, is only 14 miles) and making approximately 10 knots. He saw what he described as a "laundry basket shaped conning tower" which distinguished it from American fleet boats. His observation was particularly drawn to the extensive network of railings behind the conning tower, which was typical of the arrangement found surrounding the winter-garden of Type IXC/40 German U-boats like the *U-853*. As an unarmed training flight, they were unable to attack the target, but they immediately headed back to the Quonset NAS, landing on runway 34, where they raced to the station Admiral's office to report the sighting and to file their flight report. After a three-hour debriefing by the Air Combat Information (ACI) Officer (Bradley thought was the Admiral's aide, he believed to have been a LCDR named Monahan), their observation was dismissed as a false sighting. Little more than seven hours later, however, their sighting would prove to have been accurate, though their flight log (known by the flight crews as the so-called "yellow sheet") seems to have disappeared from the official Navy records of that day. It is probably not surprising that such documentation might have been redacted from daily log, as *VC-15* was seen a "visiting" training squadron that raised a legitimate alarm that was simply ignored by the authorities at the Quonset NAS in the closing days of the war. Furthermore, according to Nathaniel Patch, Archivist, Archives II Reference Section (RDT2) at the National Archives at College Park, Maryland:

> According to the Navy's Records Management Manual (SECNAV 5201.1), the only logs that are retained as permanent records are the deck logs of commissioned

US Naval vessels. Other logs including flight and station logs are not retained as permanent records.

At 5:35 PM on Saturday, 5 May 1945, several merchant vessels were plying the waters off of Narragansett Bay, Rhode Island, including the aged 368 foot, 5,353 ton collier S.S. *Black Point.* Built in 1918 and owned by the C. H. Sprague & Son Steamship Company, of Boston, the S.S. *Black Point,* under command of Captain Charles E. Prior of Belfast, Maine, was steaming Northeast for the Edison power plant at the L Street wharf in South Boston, via the intracoastal waterways of Long Island Sound, Rhode Island Sound, and the Cape Cod Canal. The non-zigzagging, unescorted *Black Point* carrying a 7,759 ton cargo of soft bituminous Virginia coal, was making 8 knots at a position approximately 3.7 miles Southeast of Point Judith, Rhode Island, off the West entrance of Narragansett Bay. At the same time, a tanker, two small freighters and a tug boat towing several barges navigated the waters nearby. Without warning and in an attack hauntingly similar to that employed against the *PE-56,* a T-5 passive-acoustic homing torpedo launched by the submerged *U-853* caused a tremendous explosion which tore off forty feet of the *Black Point*'s stern, severing her propeller, rudder and 4-inch/50-caliber deck gun mount aft of her number 5 cargo hold.

Captain Prior had been standing on the *Black Point*'s bridge and was just about to light a Camel cigarette when the explosion occurred. His first thought was that his ship had struck a mine. Merchant crewman Joseph Raymond Tharl, later recalled that he had been below decks, eating their regular Saturday dinner of franks and beans in the galley amidships, when the torpedo struck. He raced to the radio room and started transmitting an S.O.S. radio distress signal, as Captain Prior struggled to pry the stunned Third Mate, Homer Small's hands from the ship's helm. Captain Prior then rushed to secure the ship's records, and gave the order to abandon ship. In the excitement and confusion following the explosion, several sailors were crushed and injured, or killed as lifeboats swung wildly from their davits, and Captain Prior insisted on being the last man to leave his ship. The *Black Point*'s small stern section quickly sank in 78 feet of water at 41 degrees 19.02' North, 71 degrees 25.01' West, as the larger 230 foot long bow section drifted into deeper water as it settled by the stern, rolled over to port then capsized and sank to the bottom at 5:55 PM. Eleven crewmen and one U.S. Navy armed guard went down with the ship, with 34 survivors rescued by nearby vessels (see Appendix IV). The S.S. *Black Point* was the last American flagged merchant ship to be torpedoed by a German U-boat during the war.

The 296 foot, 1,551 ton Swedish flagged Norwegian Svenska Lloyd, Rederiaktiebolaget Line freighter S.S. *Scandinavia*, and the antiquated 312 foot, 2,541 ton Yugoslavian "Alcesu" Parobrodarsko Drustovo SOJ Line tramp steamer S.S. *Karmen* (erroneously listed as S.S. *Kamen* in many sources), witnessed the explosion and approached to pick up the survivors who were later transferred to the 83 foot U.S. Coast Guard patrol craft U.S.C.G.C. *Hibiscus*, and the 180 foot seagoing buoy tender U.S.C.G.C. *Hornbeam* (W-394), from Point Judith, and two U.S. Navy crash boats from Newport, Rhode Island.

Immediately following the explosion aboard the S.S. *Black Point*, the *U-853* once again mysteriously surfaced, this time for a few minutes. Officers and crewmen aboard the S.S. *Karmen* witnessed the *U-853* surface, and saw several crewmen momentarily appear on her aft deck. Strangely, witnesses aboard the steamer indicated the U-boat crewmen appeared to be attempting to deploy a yellow inflatable life raft, or to retrieve something from the water. The *U-853* crewmen soon scrambled back down the hatches, however, and the U-boat quickly dove from view as the Captain of the S.S. *Karmen* sent out an S.O.S. radio distress transmission at 5:42 PM. The transmission was received by several nearby U.S. Navy and Coast Guard warships steaming approximately 30 miles away, approaching the Southwest end of the Cape Cod Canal in Buzzard's Bay, heading for the Boston Navy Shipyard for repairs and provisions after escorting elements of the 80 ship convoy GUS-84 from Gibraltar to Norfolk, Philadelphia, and New York. Within 2 hours of sinking the S.S. *Black Point*, the submerged *U-853* was being hunted by the U.S. Navy destroyer escorts U.S.S. *Amick* (*DE-168*), U.S.S. *Atherton* (*DE-169*), U.S.S. *Booth* (*DE-170*), and the U.S. Coast Guard manned Tacoma class frigate U.S.S. (U.S.C.G.) *Moberly* (*PF-63*), of Hunter/Killer Task Group 60.7, later assisted by the destroyer U.S.S. *Ericsson* (*DD-440*), and two U.S. Navy blimps.

Other U.S. Navy warships including the U.S.S. *Action* (*PG-86*), U.S.S. *Barney* (*DD-149*), U.S.S. *Breckenridge* (*DD-148*), U.S.S. *Blakely* (*DD-150*), U.S.S. *Newport* (*PF-27*), U.S.S. *Restless* (*PG-66*), and the U.S.S. *Semmes* (*AG-24*), formerly the flush-deck destroyer (*DD-189*), soon arrived on scene and established a barrier patrol around the search area to prevent the U-boat from escaping her hunters.

Simultaneously, further to the South, elements of the escort-carrier U.S.S. *Card's* (*CVE-11*) Carrier Task Unit (CTU) 28.22 operating in the "Carqual Area" (Carrier Qualification area), including the destroyers U.S.S. *Baldwin* (*DD-624*), U.S.S. *Frankford* (*DD-497*) and U.S.S. *Nelson* (*DD-623*), received a dispatch from the Commander Eastern Sea Frontier (CESF), to report to Carrier Task Group (CTG) 20.1 and join the hunt for the *U-853*.

While heading toward Block Island Sound, the *Baldwin*:

> reported a sound contact in 40-10N, 69-55W at 20:05 [hours]. The contact was attacked, but CTG 28.22 stated that additional runs gave negative results. CESF felt certain that this was a contact on the hull of the S/S *Pan Pennsylvania*.

The American flagged S.S. *Pan Pennsylvania* was a 504 foot, 10,017 ton T-2 type tanker owned by National Bulk Carriers, Inc., and had been torpedoed and sunk by the Type IXC/40 U-boat *U-550*

(Kapitanleutnant Klaus Hanert) on 16 April 1944 approximately 60 miles Southeast of Nantucket Island with the loss of 2 Officers, 10 armed guards and 13 crewmen.

Back at the *U-853*, the relatively shallow waters and flat bottom topography of Rhode Island Sound did not offer the protective cover found off the coast of Maine, and made avoiding sonar detection by surface warships far more difficult. At 8:14 on the evening on 5 May 1945 the U.S.S. *Atherton* (LCDR, Lewis Iselin, USNR), picked up a sound contact on the *U-853* as she slowly crept South on her electric motors close to the bottom, attempting to escape detection in the deep shoals known as East Ground. At 8:29 PM the Moberly dropped 13 magnetic depth-charges on the sound contact, one of which detonated. According to Moberly Sonarman 2nd Class, Richard I. DuBurg:

> It was determined that contact was moving slowly along at course 090 degrees true and returning echo revealing a slight down doppler and the submarine screws were heard by our sound operator. Now it is Moberly's turn for the attack, dropping a thirteen depth charge pattern. Closing in on the attack area a sudden speed up of the submarine screws trying to get out of the explosive area told us they were still able to navigate.

The *Amick* (LCDR, E. L. Baraumian, USNR), was ordered to leave the scene to assist the destroyer escort U.S.S. *Booth*, in escorting another merchant freighter from New York to Boston. The *Ericsson* (LCDR, C. A. Baldwin, USN), soon arrived on scene to assist *Atherton* and *Moberly* (LCDR, Leslie B. Tollaksen, USCG), in their search and follow-up attacks on the sonar contact. The *Atherton* made two subsequent Hedgehog attacks on the target before marking the area with a lighted buoy and breaking off the attack to conduct repairs and reload her Hedgehog spigot launchers, stern mounted depth-charge racks, and depth-charge throwing Y-guns and K-guns.

Sound contact on the stricken sub was soon regained, and the three warships conducted additional attacks until evidence of a hit began to well up to the surface at approximately 11:45 PM, indicating the *U-853* had been damaged, if not destroyed. Richard DuBurg later recounted:

> After the attack our search lights in the dark revealed air bubbles and oil welling to the surface with bits of wood, cork, and dead fish, rubber inflatable raft, lifejackets tied in knots, wooden flagstaff, a pillow with an embroidered duck on the corner, the Captain's cap and a whiskey wood crate marked Kesserling.

On the morning on 6 May 1945, two ZNP type U.S. Navy blimps K-16 (Lt. jg, J. T. Clark, USNR), and K-58 (Lt. jg, M. I. Zabst, USNR), out of Lakehurst, New Jersey, arrived on scene to search the area of the debris field and diesel oil slick. They made a strong contact on the *U-853* with their MAD gear, and marked the position with dye markers and a smoke buoy. The shallow depth of the bottomed target required the attacking warships to set their depth-charges fitted with hydrostatic detonators, for only 75 to 100 feet, to insure they would have sufficient depth to detonate before hitting bottom. These shallow depth settings caused the depth-charges to detonate dangerously close to the warships, requiring them to increase their attack speed from 15 to 18+ knots. The tremendous concussion still resulted in damage to their steering-gear and delicate instruments, however, particularly their sound gear and navigational equipment. One after another, the *Atherton*, *Moberly* and *Ericsson*, each made successive passes over the *U-853*, conducting depth-charge and Hedgehog attacks on the bottomed target before drifting-off to repair damaged equipment. According to Richard DuBurg:

> The following morning, Saturday, May 6th, our Captain decided we were going to put a final end to the

sucker and ordered a hedgehog 24 rocket bow attack followed through with a firing and drop of 13 depth charge pattern. When a battery of 24 hedgehogs were fired out from the bow of a ship the sonar officer who now has the conn as it is known for steering, bearing and speed immediately calls for a left or right rudder, depending on which direction opposite of the sub travels to be out of the resulting explosive zone. This action was against all ethics of anti-submarine warfare. Sonar officer J.G. George Racraft looked at me and remarked: "did you hear over the intercom the order from the Captain?" I said yes, call for verification and it came through and I said, "we can not do that, he is crazy." We fired our battery of 24 hedgehogs and followed over that sinking pattern with a thirteen depth charge pattern. The results were a tremendous underwater explosion under our ship which felt like it raised up out of the water. Our ship came to a halt not too far from the sub location shutting down the engines, all electrical power, steering damage, broken pipes, lights out, crew thrown about and dust flew out of every crack, etc., and we had to stand off for repairs.

The trapped *U-853*, lying dead on the bottom, underwent a 16 hour long deluge of more than 20 successive Hedgehog and depth-charge attacks during which approximately 30 tons of explosives were dropped on the crippled U-boat, including 195 depth-charges, 264 Hedgehogs and 6 retro-bombs. These attacks brought a great deal of diesel oil and wreckage to the surface, including Drager (tauchretter) escape lungs (similar to the U.S. Navy's "Momsen Lung"), inflatable life rafts, life jackets, abandon ship kits (each containing a canteen of fresh water, food rations and a one-man life-raft), rubber foul-weather gear and assorted debris including cork (used in the U-boat's insulation), the wooden flagstaff from the railing aft of the wintergarden, and Commander Frömsdorf's Officer's cap and chart table. The blimp *K-16* dropped a sonobuoy on the spreading oil slick, and both it and the *K-58* monitored sounds described as "rhythmic hammering on a metal surface, which was interrupted periodically." The blimps directed whaleboats to collect surfacing debris, and conducted several attacks on the stationary target with their 7.2 inch rocket-propelled "retro-bomb" depth-bombs. At 10:45 on the morning of 6 May 1945, the Commander of Task Group 60.7 (CDR, F. C. B. McCune, USN), embarked aboard the *Ericsson*, declared the U-boat "sunk and on the bottom." The U.S. Navy's experimental sound-training ship U.S.S. *Semmes (AG-24)* closed on the target with her new XQHA type sonar, marking the wreck with buoys.

On the afternoon of 6 May 1945 the U.S. Navy submarine tender/rescue ship U.S.S. *Penguin (ASR-12)* out of the New London, Connecticut, Submarine Base arrived on scene, and U.S. Navy hard-hat diver, Edwin J. R. Bockelman, descended to inspect and identify the wreck of the stricken U-boat. He landed on the submarine's conning tower and found the hatch crammed with the bodies of several German naval Officers and crewmen wearing escape equipment. Despite the danger of numerous unexploded depth-charges and Hedgehogs surrounding the wreck, he recovered the body of one dead crewman (Matrosenobergefreiter or Seaman 2nd Class Herbert Hoffmann 04.09.22), from the conning tower as evidence of the "kill," credited to the *Atherton*, with all 55 Officers and crewmen aboard the *U-853*, lost (see Appendix V). Navy diver Bockelman identified the stricken U-boat by her number *U-853*, as he witnessed it painted on her conning tower insignia.

On 7 May 1945 the U.S. Navy dispatched the coastal minesweeper U.S.S. *Acme (AMc-61)* under Commander (Ensign) Oliver Littleton, to stand station over the wreck of the *U-853*, and to remain there in the event that any of her crewmen were still alive, and to rescue them in the event they attempted to make the dangerous ascent from the stricken U-boat. The *Acme* fouled her 300 pound Danforth anchor on the wreck of the *U-853*, and later that evening heavy seas caused her to part her anchor chain, leaving her anchor embedded in the starboard side of the U-boat below her conning tower, and several fathoms of anchor chain draped over the wreck. The *Acme* returned to Newport, Rhode Island, leaving the wreck of the *U-853* and her dead Officers and crewmen, to fade into history. The unconditional surrender of Germany took place the next day, on 8 May 1945. The wreck of the *U-853* lies in 130 feet of water approximately 6.8 miles East of Block Island, Rhode Island, at 41 degrees 14.3' North; 71 degrees 25.2' West. Many of the secrets of *U-853*'s activities on her final patrol lie entombed within her rusting hull, along with the remains of her long lost Officers and crewmen.

After five years and eight months,
the final chapter of the Battle of the Atlantic,
the longest and bloodiest naval engagement in world history,
had finally come to an end.

The U-Boat War's Final Toll

The Battle of the Atlantic began two days after Germany's September 1st 1939 invasion of Poland, when, on September 3rd of 1939, the same day Great Britain declared war on Germany, the German Type VII U-boat *U-30*, under the command of Kapitanleutnant Fritz-Julius Lemp, torpedoed and sank the British passenger liner H.M.S. *Athenia*. For more than 5 years and 8 months the deadliest naval battle in history raged across the Atlantic Ocean. The last U-boat to sink Allied shipping during the war was the *U-2336*, a Type XXIII U-boat under the command of Kapitanleutnant Emil Klausmeier on May 7th 1945 East of Dunbar, Scotland. The ships he torpedoed were the diminutive, 280 foot, 1,791 ton Norwegian flagged S.S. *Sneland I*, and the 2,878 ton Canadian flagged S.S. *Avondale Park*. The *U-2335* returned to Kiel, Germany, and surrendered on May 14th 1945. Technically, it can be argued that the Battle of the Atlantic did not officially end until the last German U-boat, the *U-977* under command of Oberleutnant zur See Heinz Schaffer, surrendered at Mar del Plata, Argentina, on August 17th 1945, more that three months after Germany's surrender (and three days after the official surrender of Japan).

During the war, Germany's Kriegsmarine fired nearly **38,000** torpedoes, for which its U-boats were credited with the sinking or destruction of **2,828** Allied and neutral vessels including merchant freighters, tankers, military transports, passenger liners and **176** Allied warships, totaling more than **14,300,000** gross tons. Of the **1,162** German U-boats of varying types commissioned during the war, **784** were sunk or destroyed. Some **429** of those U-boats were sunk without any survivors, with **215** U-boats lost on their first war patrol. Of more than **39,000** German Kriegsmarine Officers and crewmen to serve in the U-boat service during the war, approximately **28,000** were killed and **5,000** captured, an attrition rate greater than **80+%**, higher than that sustained by any branch of any major combatant nations' military services during the war. The U.S. merchant fleet alone lost more than **700** ships sunk, with the loss of more than **5,600** merchant Officers and crewmen, while the British merchant fleet lost more than **30,000** men killed in the German U-boat campaign. Conservative estimates of the casualties incurred during the Battle of the Atlantic exceed **80,000** lives lost, including all of the Axis and Allied naval personnel, airmen, troops, merchant crewmen and civilians lost to the cold, dark depths.

Postscript

In March of 1998 the author met with friends, Brockton, Massachusetts firemen Bob and Paul Westerlund, and discussed the mysterious circumstances surrounding the sinking of the U.S.S. *Eagle 56*, and the death of their father, Seaman 2nd Class, Ivar A. Westerlund. That meeting led to a two-decade-long search for survivors, witnesses, German and U.S. Navy records and other evidence to establish the true cause of the 23 April 1945 loss of the *PE-56*. In July of 2000 the author and a group of dedicated volunteers organized and conducted a side-scan sonar search for the long lost wreck of the *PE-56* off the coast of Cape Elizabeth, Maine. In September of 2000, the late Massachusetts Congressman John Joseph "Joe" Moakley (1927 to Memorial Day 28 May 2001), petitioned the Secretary of the U.S. Navy (SECNAV), for an investigation into the loss of the *PE-56*. Former SECNAV Admiral Richard Danzig, assigned the case back to the U.S. Navy Judge Advocate General (JAG), who declined to re-open the Court of Inquiry. The SECNAV and JAG then referred the matter to the U.S. Navy Historical Center at Washington, DC, where former Deputy Director of Naval History Captain Marshall A. Hall, assigned the case for review by a team of their best archivists and researchers headed by Senior Archivist Bernard Cavalcante.

After reviewing all of the evidence regarding this incident, in May of 2001 the Director of Naval History Dr. William S. Dudley, made a formal Recommendation to Chief of Naval Operations (CNO) Admiral Vernon E. Clark, and subsequently to then recently appointed SECNAV, Gordon England, that the official record regarding the loss of the U.S.S. *Eagle 56*, be changed to "enemy action." On 26 June

2001 Secretary England signed that Recommendation, and the U.S. Navy officially changed the cause for the loss of the *PE-56*, to enemy action by the German U-boat, *U-853*, fifty-six years after the fact.

In a formal ceremony at the U.S. Navy Shipbuilding Museum aboard the U.S.S. *Salem* (*CA-139*) in Quincy, Massachusetts, on Saturday, the 8th of June 2002, the U.S. Navy awarded fifty-one (51) Purple Heart Medals, and other decorations and awards to the casualties of the U.S.S. *Eagle 56*, forty-nine (49) posthumously.

Soon after the Purple Heart ceremony aboard the U.S.S. *Salem*, the author and the Westerlund brothers met to discuss the possibility of raising private funds to place a fitting memorial marker on the grounds of Fort Williams at Cape Elizabeth, Maine, to commemorate the Officers and crewmen of the U.S.S. *Eagle PE-56*. They created a non-profit organization and mailed letters to the families and friends of all of the men of the *PE-56* who had been located up to that time. Within just a few months they had raised the funds necessary for the fabrication and construction of a beautiful bronze and granite memorial marker.

On Saturday, April 23, 2005, the 60th Anniversary of the sinking of the U.S.S. *Eagle PE-56*, the author, along with the Westerlund brothers, the three living survivors of the sinking, John Scagnelli, John Breeze and Harold Petersen, their families and the families of approximately a dozen deceased Officers and crewmen met at Portland Head Light at Cape Elizabeth, Maine, to dedicate a memorial marker to the *PE-56* Officers and crewmen. A Barre-gray, Vermont granite stone inlaid with a bronze plaque showing the bas-relief profile of the U.S.S. *Eagle PE-56* was unveiled on the cliff walk approximately 290 feet to the South of the lighthouse, overlooking the Atlantic Ocean, where the *PE-56* had exploded and sunk 60 years earlier. Beneath the profile of the ship reads the following inscription:

IN MEMORY OF THE OFFICERS AND CREWMEN OF THE
U.S. NAVY'S EAGLE CLASS SUB-CHASER

U.S.S EAGLE 56 (PE-56)

TORPEDOED AND SUNK BY THE GERMAN U-BOAT U-853
APPROXIMATELY NINE MILES SOUTHEAST OF THIS
LOCATION ON MONDAY 23 APRIL 1945 WITH THE LOSS OF
FORTY-NINE OFFICERS AND CREWMEN.
THIRTEEN SURVIVORS WERE RESCUED.
THE GREATEST LOSS OF U.S. NAVY PERSONNEL
IN NEW ENGLAND WATERS DURING WORLD WAR II.

Following our initial search for the wreck of the U.S.S. *Eagle PE-56* in July of 2000, Internationally renowned side-scan sonar expert Garry Kozak returned to Casco Bay on more than a dozen occasions, widening his search of the sea floor for the elusive shipwreck. By 2018 Kozak had mapped approximately 37 square miles of Casco Bay, locating several other wrecks, but not that of the *PE-56*. Ultimately, Kozak realized the wreck could not have simply vanished, but likely lay somewhere near the original search coordinates, possibly eluding detection because of the highly irregular bottom topography of complex geographic [rock] outcroppings and other naturally occurring anomalies. After nearly two decades of fruitless searches, the elusive wreck of the *PE-56* had become known by the technical shipwreck diving community as the "Gray Ghost of the Atlantic Coast."

In or about 2014 the Nomad Exploration [Deep Dive] Team, using coordinates provided to them by this author, employed the assistance of Garry Kozak, to continue the search for the wreckage of the *PE-56*. The Nomad Team consisted of divers: Ryan King, Jeff Goudreau, Bob Foster, Danny Allan, Mark Bowers, Don Ferrara, Nate Garrett, and Josh Cummings. For the next several years, the team repeatedly dove to investigate previously unidentified bottom anomalies located by Kozak.

On Saturday, June 23, 2018, the Nomad Team discovered the bow of the *PE-56* with its distinctive 4-inch deck gun in more that 250 feet of water, within a quarter of a mile from where the original search team started their search in 2000. Upon surfacing from that historic dive, Diver Danny Allan called this author to decribe their discovery. The diver's reported that approximately 20 feet of the bow had broken off from the rest of the forward half of the wreck of the *PE-56*, and was lying on its port side on the sea floor. Some speculated that the damage to the bow occurred when the wreck struck bottom, but the author is convinced this was not the case. Witness accounts clearly show the bow sank by the amidships, and would have landed on the sea floor in the same orientation. The damage to the bow has a much simpler explanation, having more to do with the Eagle boats' construction rather than battle damage, or impacting with the sea floor.

One unique feature of the Eagle boats' design reflected back to the late 19th and early 20th centuries, the idea of the ramming bow. The idea or ships ramming other ships to hole their hulls and sink them actually dates back several millennia, as reinforces metal rams were affixed to the bows of ancient wood hulled galleys deployed by the Greeks and Romans. The Eagle class boats possessed an extremely sharp, pointed bow, which dropped straight down at a right angle to the keel, looking much like an axe blade. The U.S. Navy had Ford reinforce the bows of the Eagle boats to create the perfect ramming weapon, by sealing the bow compartment off with a solid bulkhead and filling the void with concrete. In doing so, they turned the bow of the Eagle boats into giant can openers, capable or tearing open a surfaced U-boat's thick pressure hull if the opportunity arose. The damage to the wreck of the *PE-56*'s bow was obviously the result of the tremendous weight of the concrete reinforced ramming bow, which caused the hull plates to weaken over more than seven decades submerged in salt water, and the bow to break away.

On Saturday, August 11, 2018, Nomad Team diver Bob Foster called to advise this author that they had just located the stern of the *PE-56* in approximately 250 feet of water just 300 feet from the bow, conclusively identifying it by the presence of late WWII era Mark IX "treardrop" shaped depth charges in the stern racks. The dive team also reported finding dozens, if not hundreds of old Coca-Cola® bottles strewn around the stern of the *PE-56* wreck. The author shared with them this anecdote that might explain the origin of those scattered soda bottles:

> Since we operated out of Key West [1944] there was one misery everyone shared, officers included—the pervasive heat. Air conditioning just didn't exist for us. Everyone suffered from heat rash. The sea temperature was above 80 degrees F and since our potable water was in an inner tank, it too was above 80 degrees. Except when the distilling unit was discharging into it. Then the temperature of our drinking water was more like 100 degrees, but we could depend on our water cooler to bring it down to almost 80 degrees when we wanted a drink of "cold" water. Fortunately, we had a Coke machine. It was located on the main deck aft and consisted of an ice-filled tank bearing a Coca-Cola logo. Our operating circumstances were such that we could get ice from ashore often enough to avoid a mutiny.
>
> —By former Eagle boat crewman, Lou Chirillo, "This Eagle Wasn't Flying," *U.S. Naval Institute Proceedings* magazine, Summer 1990

Apparently, the crew would stow the returnable Coke bottles in one of the many wooden storage boxes along the railings on the aft deck, and after decades submerged, the storage boxes deteriorated, releasing the bottles to be scattered about the stern of the wreck. Another mystery solved.

On Friday, May 31, 2019 at 1:58 PM this author received a call from Nomad Team diver, Jeff Goodreau, to say that they had just surfaced from the wreck site and that they had located and extensively photographed both boilers, lying next to each other, on their sides, fully intact! The three drums and hundreds of interconnected water-tubes of both boilers all appeared to have been undamaged, as conclusive forensic evidence that the boilers did not explode, and therefore did not cause the sinking of the *PE-56*. The Nomad Deep Dive Team's non-invasive, photographic survey of the wreck of the *PE-56* was conducted in a dignified manner, showing great respect for that sacred war grave. The U.S. Navy recognized their findings and thanked the Team for their work, further corroborating that the ship was sunk in an act of combat.

The discovery of the wreck of the U.S.S. *Eagle PE-56*, her boilers and the forensic evidence derived therefrom conclusively confirmed the author's assessment of the documentary evidence and witness statements concerning the sinking of that ship. The *PE-56* exploded, broke in half and sank as the result of an external, underwater force that could only have come from the detonation of a large explosive device. Since the German U-boat *U-853* was known to have been operating in the vicinity at that time, that it had actually been spotted by the *PE-56* survivors, and because no U-boats had deployed mines anywhere near that area, it is an obvious conclusion that the U.S.S. *Eagle PE-56* was sunk by a torpedo launched by the *U-853*, and that her Officers and crewmen were in fact, lost "Due to Enemy Action."

On 2 May 2020, just a week following the 75th Anniversary of the sinking of the USS *Eagle PE-56*, the Author along with the Westerlund brothers, the families of the Officers and crewmen of the PE-56 and the members of the Nomad Dive Team, met at Portland Head Light at Cape Elizabeth, Maine, to dedicate a second memorial marker. This marker was installed immediately next to the original marked dedicated on the 60th Anniversary of the sinking, but included all of the names, ranks and rates of the Officers and crewmen, those killed and the survivors of the sinking of the *PE-56*.

The Salvage of the *U-853*:
Desecration of a War Grave

Under international law, wrecks of warships remain the property of the sovereign nation under whose flag they sailed. Furthermore, warship wrecks that contain the remains of their Officers or crewmen are considered war graves, and are to be protected by the nation in whose waters they lie. Such vessels are not to be salvaged, desecrated, nor disturbed in any way. Those international laws and treaties, however, have proven not to be sufficient to protect such wrecks and war graves as the German U-boat *U-853*, from being pillaged, looted and desecrated. Salvagers and recreational divers have been picking over the wreck of the *U-853* for more than half a century, disturbing and removing human remains, the personal effects of her Officers and crewmen, historical artifacts, and destroying the sanctity and archaeological integrity of the war grave site.

Immediately following the destruction of the *U-853*, on the afternoon of 6 May 1945 the U.S. Navy submarine tender/rescue ship U.S.S. *Penguin* (*ASR-12*) arrived on scene, and U.S. Navy hard-hat diver, Edwin J. R. Bockelman, descended to inspect and identify the wreck of the stricken U-boat. He recovered the body of one dead crewman (Matrosenobergefreiter, or Seaman 2nd Class, Herbert Hoffmann; DOB: September 4, 1922; Service # UO 28177-41S), from the conning tower of the submarine as evidence of the "kill."

Herbert Hoffman's body was transferred from the *Penguin* to a smaller vessel and brought to the U.S. Naval Submarine Base, New London, at Groton, Connecticut, accompanied by U.S. Navy Lieutenant Commander Ira Dye, who was allegedly taking part in a classified project involving the *U-853*. That classified project simply involved the recovery of documents and equipment from sunken German U-boats for intelligence purposes.

> Because of this security classification Hoffman's body could not be given a proper military burial. The Naval Dispensary [medical clinic] would not accept the body [apparently, the duty Officer would not sign for the remains], and could not turn it over to the civilian mortuary that handled burials under government contract. The body lay in a walk-in freezer overnight in the base kitchen (mess hall), and the next morning, at dawn, a harbor vessel, along with this Navy Commander (actually Lt.Cdr. Dye) and a Catholic Chaplain (Station Chaplain, Fr. John Feeley), went out beyond the 3-mile limit. There, after giving seaman Hoffman an ecumenical burial service, his body in a weighted bag was committed to the sea off Southwest Ledge.

There was a funeral ceremony conducted for seaman Hoffman at the Newport Naval Base with full military honors, and apparently, in some cemetery in Newport there is a grave marker bearing MtrOgfr. Herbert Hoffman's name, though his mortal remains do not lie in those hallowed grounds.

Following the May 5/6th 1945 sinking of the *U-853* by U.S. Naval forces, her rusting hull remained on the bottom of Rhode Island Sound as the "iron coffin" for her long lost Officers and crewmen. By the early 1950s a number of wild rumors began to circulate about the final mission of the *U-853*, and about her alleged cargo. It was claimed that family members of several crewmen were told that prior to departing from Norway on her last patrol, that treasures were secreted aboard the *U-853*, and were supposedly sealed (allegedly welded) inside large 88mm or 105mm deck-gun shell projectiles.

It was alleged that those treasures included jewels and American Express currency that had been looted by German forces from French banks, though no apparent explanation was ever given to explain why treasure would have been placed aboard a U-boat that had been sent out on a simple combat patrol to sink Allied shipping. With a U-boat attrition rate exceeding eighty (80%) percent by the end of World War II, it would have been extremely improbable that anything of significant value would have been loaded aboard an offensive U-boat at that time, as there was little hope such cargo would ever make it to its intended destination.

Furthermore, those rumors appear to have been generated by individuals with little or no genuine knowledge about the *U-853* in particular, because she was not fitted with a traditional deck-gun as were often seen on the fore-deck of U-boats early in the war. By 1943, as the tide turned against the U-boat arm of the Kriegsmarine, the hunters had become the hunted, and surfaced deck-gun attacks against Allied shipping had grown extremely dangerous. With the introduction of comprehensive anti-submarine operations, detection equipment, increased air patrols, countermeasures and anti-submarine weapon systems, U-boats were forced to operate and attack shipping by torpedoes, while submerged. As a result, by 1944 traditional 88mm (originally mounted on Type VII boats) & 105mm (Type IX boat) deck-guns had been removed from most operational U-boats, and only relatively small 20mm & 37mm (fleigerabwehrkanone) "flak" anti-aircraft (AA) guns remained mounted on their "wintergardens," the small gun platforms mounted aft of the U-boats' conning towers. Such small caliber guns had tiny explosive charges and therefore could not be hollowed-out to accommodate any significant amounts of treasure.

Another unfounded rumor also began to circulate, that the *U-853* had been carrying a million dollar cargo of mercury sealed in stainless steel containers hidden in the boat's saddle tanks. Type IX U-boats like the *U-853* did not have saddle tanks. Another version of the rumor indicated that mercury had substituted lead ballast in the U-boat's keel duct. The origin of those rumors, though as false as claims that the *U-853* carried treasure, is more easily explained. After Germany's official surrender on 8 May 1945 many U-boats began to surrender to Allied forces, including several that surrendered to American forces and put in at the U.S. Naval Base at Portsmouth, New Hampshire. Two of those boats included the Type XB U-boat *U-234* under command of Kapitanleutnant Johann-Heinrich Fehler, and the Type IXD2 U-boat *U-873* under command of Kapitanleutnant Friedrich Steinhoff. The *U-234* had not been conducting a traditional combat patrol (to sink Allied shipping), but was a mine-laying U-boat that had been converted to a cargo-carrying U-Cruiser and was traveling to Japan with strategic materials that were desperately needed for the Japanese war effort in the Pacific. The *U-234* had been carrying a German Luftwaffe (Air Force) General (General der Flieger, Ulrich Otto Eduard Kessler), several Japanese naval (submarine & aircraft) technicians (Lieutenant Commander Hideo Tomonga and LCDR Shoji Genzo), blueprints for Germany's secret weapons, two disassembled Me-262 jet fighter aircraft, 560 kilograms (approximately 1,200 pounds), of uranium-oxide (some experts believe it was actually uranium hexafluoride), and several tons of mercury and optical glass crystals, among other items. Likewise, the *U-873* had originally been intended to carry strategic materials to Japan, but her orders were changed to that of a regular combat patrol to sink Allied shipping, just before she sailed from Norway, but before most of her cargo could be off-loaded. Once at Portsmouth, New Hampshire, the cargoes of the *U-234* and the *U-873* were off-loaded behind large, visually restrictive, green canvas tarps, by dozens of shipyard workers under heavy U.S. Marine armed guard and supervised by U.S. Naval Intelligence personnel. Those mysterious events subsequently led to the spread of groundless rumors that other U-boats operating in the last days of the war, were also carrying "mercury" and other "treasure."

The first recorded salvage attempt on the wreck of the *U-853* took place approximately 8 years after her sinking. In September of 1953 an individual named Oswald L. Bonifay of Baltimore, Maryland, began soliciting dragger-boat Captains at the piers along Thames Street in Newport, Rhode Island, for work on what he described as a secret search and salvage operation off the coast. Bonifay met up with Captain Gilbert Brownell of the dragger *Maureen* and offered him $100.00 a day "cash" plus all expenses "to do some sub hunting." Several days after the deal was closed two hard-hat divers (William George and Bill Mercer) arrived in Newport from Boston, all parties were sworn to secrecy and Bonifay produced some charts he had acquired from a friend in the Navy and blueprints and diagrams of a Type IXC/40 U-boat that he had secured from German Archives. Just two days into the search they located the wreck of the *U-853* and diving operations began on the wreck. Bonifay himself allegedly made some 17 dives on the *U-853* using the newly invented SCUBA equipment he had purchased from France. The hard-hat divers sometimes made as many as four dives (2 each per man) per day, and the operation went on for approximately 10 weeks. Rumors quickly spread around Newport waterfront, about Bonifay's strange salvage efforts on the mysterious Nazi U-boat wreck.

On November 3, 1953 Bonifay and his divers raised the *U-853*'s two manganese-bronze screw-propellers, each with 3 blades, measuring approximately 5 feet in diameter and weighing approximately 900 pounds. At some point it is alleged that Bonifay sold the propellers to local businessman J.T. O'Connell, whose family owned the Inn at Castle Hill. It is believed, however, that the deal was in part, payment for their living accommodations while Bonifay and his crew conducted the attempted salvage from Newport. According to O'Connell's grandson, J. Timothy O'Reilly, the present owner of the Inn at Castle Hill, his "grandfather owned a marine supply store and took the propellers as payment for the equipment Bonifay used." It has been rumored that Bonifay spent some $20,000.00, in the failed salvage attempt. It was only after he made another failed salvage attempt in May of 1959, that in 1961 Bonifay broke his silence and disclosed that he had been seeking a million dollars in mercury that was rumored to have been secreted aboard the boat. At that time Bonifay claimed the mercury had been aboard the *U-853* for transfer to Japan, however, it is known that she was simply conducting a traditional offensive combat patrol. Furthermore, because she was not an extreme-long-range boat, the *U-853* was in no way capable of transiting to the Far East without refueling. During Bonifay's salvage attempts it appears little salvage work had been conducted on the interior of the wreck, but that much of the external hydrodynamic hull plating had been cut or burned away. It appears that Bonifay was looking for the alleged mercury filled stainless steel containers he believed were hidden in the spaces between the external hull and the pressure hull.

The next major salvage attempt took place in 1960 when Burton H. Mason of Trumbull, Connecticut, and his 4-man dive team began searching the wreck of the *U-853* on May 6th, the 15th anniversary of her sinking. Mason's first penetrations into the interior of the wreck revealed dozens of skeletons lying about the decks, strewn with sextants, binoculars and other personal effects, an indication that Bonifay's divers had not concentrated their salvage efforts on the interior. Mason, like Bonifay, also became obsessed with the wreck, giving up his job as a heating engineer, moving to the Newport area and gambling most of his life savings in order that he could concentrate his efforts on his salvage work. Mason and his team brought up the skeletal remains of at least one crewman of the *U-853* (other sources indicate that Burton and his team brought up the remains of as many as six crewmen). Mason turned the remains over to U.S. Navy officials in Newport, who gave the German sailor(s) a burial with full military honors, but not before receiving a heated protest by the Federal Republic of West Germany's diplomatic officials in the United States. The German Consul in Boston,

Gerhard Lang, demanded that the U.S. government immediately intervene and stop Mason from further desecrating their navy's war grave, warning Mason not to disturb any more skeletal remains, nor attempt to raise the U-boat. At that time the Naval authorities of the Federal Republic of West Germany confirmed that: "Only the normal amount of mercury maintained for the operation of any submarine, and no surplus amounts, were aboard [the *U-853*]." In October of 1960 the unidentified skeletal remains of the crewman that was recovered from the *U-853* by Mason and his team, were buried in a Newport cemetery.

In 1968 the West German government apparently entered into an agreement with the Murphy Pacific Marine Salvage Company of New York and Emeryville, California, and Melvin L. Joseph Recovery Corp. of Georgetown, Delaware, to raise the wreck of the *U-853*. Apparently, the West German government gave permission to Melvin Joseph to do what it wished with the wreck, but that the remains of her crew and their personal effects be turned over to the West German government for proper disposition. According to German Naval Attaché, Captain Paul Brasack, the *U-853* had been on a regular combat patrol to sink Allied shipping and that there had been no treasure aboard the U-boat when she was sunk. In early October on 1968 the 2,000-ton salvage ship *Curb*, under command of Captain William Dukeshire, was docked at City Pier in Newport, taking on supplies for the salvage effort. It was rumored (according to one Rhode Island newspaper), that a mysterious "Mr. DuPont" had invested $300,000.00 to fund the project. Murphy Pacific's efforts to raise the wreck of the *U-853* were unsuccessful, and the next year (1969), Melvin L. Joseph Recovery Corp. contracted with Ventures International, Inc. of Harvey, Louisiana, in another salvage attempt. Alvin Holgerson of Ventures International employed their 92 foot salvage boat *Destiny* in the second unsuccessful attempt to raise the *U-853* in October of 1969.

The July 1961 issue of *Male* magazine published an article

written by Jack Goddard entitled "Mystery of the *U-853*: Million Dollar U-boat Treasure Off Rhode Island's Coast." That magazine article contained some genuine research about the *U-853*, but was also tainted by the many false rumors of alleged "Nazi treasure" lying hidden within the wreck. Such persistent erroneous treasure tales have enticed an unending parade of treasure hunters to visit and pick over the wreck of the *U-853*, hoping to fulfill their dreams of revealing her legendary secrets.

Decades of seasonal visits by thousands of recreational divers have resulted in the progressive plundering and degradation of the wreck of the *U-853*. It was not uncommon to see dive charter boats taking divers to the wreck, outfitted with hammers, chisels, crowbars, hacksaws and lift-bags, all with the intention of taking home a piece of the historic wreck to place on their mantel, as a trophy. On July 4, 1973 firefighter and diver Earl King from Norton, Massachusetts, recovered the *U-853*'s gyrocompass from inside her conning tower. In 1981 the mooring line of the *Argus*, a salvage-tug, accidentally dislodged the *U-853*'s 37mm anti-aircraft gun's barrel and flak shield. As late as the 1990s recreational divers had rigged up an air-lift and were vacuuming out much of the silt within the wreck, exposing more skeletal remains and the personal effects of the *U-853*'s crew, much of which has been looted. Hundreds, if not thousands of artifacts and personal effects of the Officers and crewmen that are known to have been recovered from the wreck by recreational divers include: china dishes; glassware; silverware; small arms (pistols); Drager (tauchreter) escape-lungs; one-man life rafts; at least one Iron Cross and other military decorations; silver cigarette cases; canteens; sextants; charts; brass fittings; binoculars; anti-aircraft ammunition (20mm and 37mm); compartment tags; gages; fuse-panels; smoking pipes; a film container; shoes; ID tags; glasses; watches; uniform buttons; coins; and the like.

The *U-853*'s thin external hydrodynamic hull structure and wood deck planking has long since deteriorated, leaving only the thick pressure hull and tween-hull pipes, compressed air tanks, water-tight storage containers, snorkel apparatus and fittings, with the wreck now bearing little resemblance to a submarine. By the Fall of 2003 the *U-853*'s knife-like, hydrodynamic bow section had broken loose from the pressure hull and had fallen to the sea floor, exposing the U-boat's torpedo tubes. Divers in early 2004 have also reported the discovery of what appeared to be part of a torpedo lying on the upper forward casing of the *U-853*, evidence of a possible salvage attempt of one of the torpedoes from the bow torpedo room of the submarine. Also in early 2004 a worker at the Delaware Technical & Community College notified History Professor Dr. Gary Wray, of the discovery of what appeared to be a light automatic cannon overgrown by brush and weeds in a corner of the college campus. Dr. Wray tracked the 1,500 pound 20mm Mauser automatic anti-aircraft (Fleigerabwehrkanone) "Flak" cannon as having been recovered by Melvin Joseph during his salvage effort on the *U-853* in 1968. That cannon, one of two twin mounts aboard the *U-853*, has since been somewhat restored for display at the Fort Miles Historical Association Museum at the Cape Henlopen State Park in Delaware. In the spring of 2004, J. Timothy O'Reilly, the owner of the Inn at Castle Hill, gave notice of his intention to transfer possession (though not legal ownership, which remains with the Federal Republic of Germany), of the *U-853*'s two 900 pound screw propellers to the Naval War College at Newport, Rhode Island, which had allegedly promised to put them on display as a historical exhibit. That has not happened, however, as those once much visited, historic tourist attractions now remain out-of-sight and forgotten, in some naval base warehouse.

With hatches open and large blast holes through the pressure hull caused by the fusillade of exploding Hedgehogs and depth-charges, the interior of the *U-853* wreck had been flooded and accessible to sea life and scavengers since the day of her sinking. After more than seven decades on the bottom of Rhode Island Sound, the bodies of the *U-853*'s Officers and crewmen had rapidly decomposed, leaving only skeletal remains. Rusting internal fittings, deteriorated cork insulation and wood trim and furnishings had left several feet of heavy silt on the interior decks of the U-boat. Because of the continued destruction of the *U-853*'s hull by recreational divers, and the removal of tons of silt from her interior, which had acted to slow her degradation, however, the U-boat's remains are more rapidly deteriorating. It may now be a matter of just a few more decades before the historic wreck and war grave of the *U-853* is rendered to little more than a pile of rust and twisted metal, to be slowly consumed by the shifting sands of Rhode Island Sound.

Modern International Treaties, Federal and State Laws to Protect Historic Shipwrecks and Sunken Military Craft

In recent years the underwater archaeological community has prevailed upon individual states, the federal government and a number foreign nations to take seriously the preservation and protection of our underwater heritage, historic shipwrecks and sunken military craft, particularly those that are war graves. Though international treaties, federal and state laws have proliferated with those noble goals in mind, in far too many cases those laws and treaties have not been vigorously enforced, allowing valuable underwater archaeological resources to be exploited, plundered and desecrated in the name of profit, or mere trophy hunting.

In the U.S., most states have established divisions or boards of underwater historical or archaeological resources that govern inland bodies of water, waterways and coastal zones generally extending out to 3 miles from shore at the mean low (tide zone) water mark. The federal government generally exercises jurisdiction of its coastal waters under the United Nations Convention on the Law of the Sea out to 12 miles from land, but for enforcement of international fisheries treaties and the like, have extended those boundaries under such names as the "Contiguous Zone" which extends out to 24 miles, the "Exclusive Economic Zone" which extends out from the base line to a maximum of 200 miles, and many coastal nations claim, and exercise sovereignty and control of all underwater resources out to their contiguous continental shelf.

The United Nations Educational, Scientific and Cultural

Organization (UNESCO) drafted an international convention for the protection of underwater cultural heritage in 2001. It is estimated that there are as many as 3 million shipwrecks spread across the ocean floors around the planet, and signatory nations have agreed to monitor and protect those historic shipwrecks and other significant archaeological resources within their respective territorial waters.

The United States Congress passed the Sunken Military Craft Act (10 U.S.C. 113) under the Federal Historic Preservation Act (SMCA) which was enacted on October 28, 2004. The primary purpose of the SMCA is to preserve and protect from unauthorized disturbance all sunken military craft that are owned by the United States government, as well as foreign sunken craft that lie within U.S. waters. Pursuant to the SMCA, the Navy's sunken military craft remain the property of the U.S. regardless of their location or the passage of time, and may not be disturbed without the permission of the U.S. Navy.

Though all of those international conventions and treaties, and national and state laws and statutes have been enacted for the purpose of protecting valuable historical underwater resources such as shipwrecks, and military war graves in particular, few instances of legitimate enforcement and prosecution have been recorded, as time and time again such wrecks are regularly plundered, looted, and desecrated for profitable salvage such as metal reclamation, and scavenged by recreational divers hunting for souvenirs.

Some of the most egregious examples of such activities have taken place in recent years in the South Pacific where entire shipwrecks have simply disappeared. In 2016 the Dutch Ministry of Defense reported that the wrecks of its cruisers, and war graves, the HNLMS *De Ruiter* (6,545 tons), and HNLMS *Java* (6,670 tons), as well as their destroyer HNLMS *Kortenaer* (1,316 tons) were found to be "missing" during a expedition to mark the 75th anniversary of the Battle of the Java Sea. A number of British, Australian and American ships have also apparently been "salvaged" for their precious metal content, including the British cruiser HMS *Exeter* (8,390 tons), the destroyer HMS *Encounter* (1,405 tons), the HMS *Electra* (1,405 tons), as well as one U.S. Navy submarine wreck. The Battle of the Java Sea took place on 27 February 1942 with the loss of 10 Allied ships and 2,173 sailors. The Australian 7,150 ton cruiser HMAS *Perth* (*D 29*) and the 9,200 ton U.S. Navy cruiser U.S.S. *Huston* (*CA-30*) survived the Battle of the Java Sea but were sunk soon thereafter, on 1 March 1942 in the Battle of Sunda Strait. Recent surveys on the *Perth* revealed that as much as 3,000 tons of metal have been removed from that wreck, and the wreck of the nearby *Houston* has also been compromised. It is believed that as many as 40 WWII era ships have been partially or completely salvaged in that area.

It is believed that those extensive, covert salvage operations were undertaken for the recovery of valuable so-called "low-background" or "pre-atomic-age" metals including steel, lead, and copper alloys. Such metals that were foundered prior to the first atmospheric atomic bomb detonation in July of 1945, have been isolated from increased amounts of atmospheric radiation. Those uncontaminated metals are vital for the production of certain finely calibrated scientific and medical devices such as Geiger counters, medical scanners, aeronautical and space sensors, and are therefore highly valuable commodities. The value of mere scrap metal alone would not otherwise justify the expense of such costly underwater recovery operations.

To date, no one has been prosecuted, nor brought to justice for the desecration and theft of those historic shipwrecks and war graves. It appears that all of the international treaties the United Nations can muster have had little or no effect on this disturbing trade.

Though the United States has done absolutely nothing to protect foreign war graves within its territorial waters, such as the plundering of the wreck of the *U-853* just off the Rhode Island coast, the families of the men lost aboard the U.S.S. *Eagle 56* (*PE-56*) hope for aggressive monitoring and protection of that hallowed U.S. Navy war grave.

Being just outside of the jurisdictional waters under the control of the state of Maine, it is still well within even the minimum (12 mile) jurisdictional boundaries of the federal government. As such, the U.S. Coast Guard should monitor all activities in the vicinity of the wreck of the *PE-56* to protect it from pilfering and desecration as a historic naval shipwreck and war grave. Because the wreck of the *PE-56* is also festooned with thousand of pounds of unexploded ordnance, Congress should act by establishing an exclusion zone around the wreck site, preventing all activities in the area, including but not limited to commercial and recreational diving. Restriction of access to the wreck of the *PE-56* would not only protect it from potential salvage and desecration, but more importantly would prevent it from becoming a source for the acquisition of thousands of pounds of high explosives by individuals with potential terroristic intent, in the interests of national security.

A similar "exclusion zone" was established approximately 30 miles to the Southwest, off the Isles of Shoals, New Hampshire, where the WWII era wreck of the 7,144 ton British freighter M/V *Empire Knight* ran aground and broke up on Boon Island Ledge on February 11, 1944 with a wartime cargo including several tons of poisonous mercury. Due to the fear that commercial salvage operations might disturb and disperse the mercury into the highly profitable bottom fishing grounds of Jeffreys Ledge on the Northern edge of the Stellwagen Bank Marine Sanctuary, a one mile diameter exclusion zone has since been established, and is strictly enforced by the United States Coast Guard. In order to protect the sanctity and integrity of the wreck of the U.S.S. *Eagle PE-56*, a similar exclusion zone should be established around that hallowed war grave site as well.

Engineering Officer, Lieutenant (jg) John Scagnelli (standing, middle row, far left), and NCO, Chief Robert Lemmon (standing, middle row, far right) with the members of the so-called "black gang" who manned the fire (boiler) room and engine room aboard the U.S.S. *Eagle* (*PE-56*). Among these men were three of the last living survivors of the ship sinking including Lt. Scagnelli, MM2c John Breeze (standing, middle row 3rd from left), and (crouching, front row 2nd from left), MM1c Harold Petersen (courtesy of John Scagnelli).

The U.S. Navy Officers and crewmen in formation on the stern
of the U.S.S. *Eagle 56* (*PE-56*), during the Change-of-Command
Ceremony at the Portland, Maine Navy Base on January 23, 1945,
exactly three months to the day before the loss of the *PE-56*.
Commander (Lt. jg) John L. Barr, (standing center) reads the
Change-of-Command Order, as he transfers command of the ship
to Lieutenant Commander James G. Early (standing to the right
of Captain Barr). Lt. Cdr. Barr requested a transfer to the Pacific
theater to "see enemy action against the Japanese." Lieutenant John
P. Scagnelli is standing to the right of Lt. Barr, facing left (courtesy
of John Scagnelli).

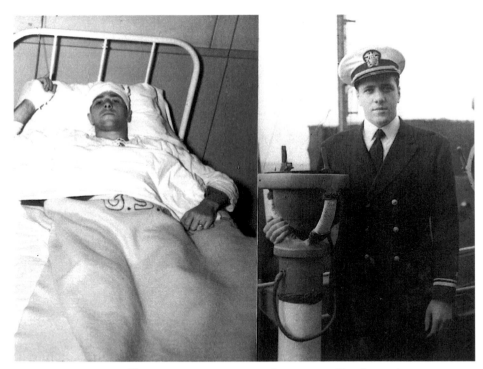

Engineering Officer, Lieutenant (jg) John Scagnelli, the only surviving Officer, and the only survivor from the bow half of the U.S.S. *Eagle* (*PE-56*), standing at the gyro compass binnacle next to the bridge of the *PE-56* (right), and recovering from injuries sustained in the explosion (left), at the Grand Trunk Naval Dispensary in Portland, Maine (courtesy of John Scagnelli).

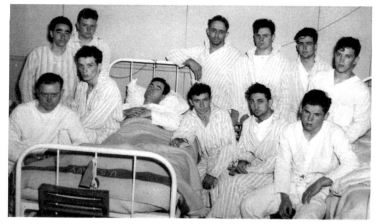

The twelve enlisted crewmen survivors of the sinking of the *PE-56*. Including Lt. Scagnelli, they were called the "Lucky 13" by the press. MM2c John Breeze is sitting on the bed at left, MM1c Harold Petersen is standing, far right. They are at the Grand Trunk Naval Dispensary at Portland, Maine, where they were held, incommunicado, for ten days following the sinking (courtesy of Harold Petersen).

The Type IXC/40 W.W.II era German U-boat *U-853* at her commissioning on 25 June 1943. Her original Commander, Kapitanleutnant Helmut Sommer is seen standing on deck, bottom row, 5th from the right with the white dress belt. Oberleutnant zur See Helmut Frömsdorf, is to the right of Commander Sommer, wearing a white dress belt and hanging ceremonial dagger (courtesy of the U-boot Archiv).

Officers and crewmen of the Type IXC/40 German U-boat *U-853*,
celebrating before their departure from Stavanger, Norway, on
their second and final patrol. Replacement Commanding Officer,
23-year-old Oberleutnant zur See (Lieutenant, Senior Grade)
Helmut Frömsdorf is at top, right, with the neck tie (courtesy of
the U-boot Archiv).

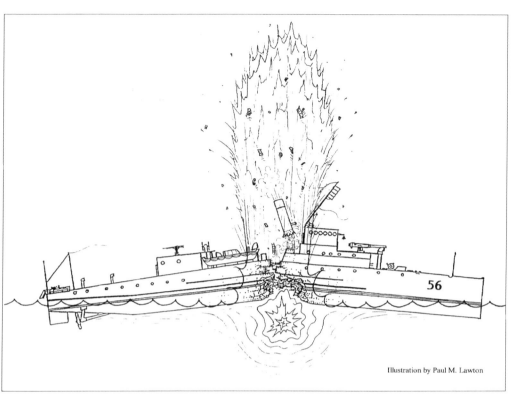

Illustration by Paul M. Lawton

The author, Paul Lawton's illustration of the catastrophic underwater explosion that lifted the U.S.S. *Eagle PE-56* out of the water, broke her keel and split her in half, sending her to the bottom within minutes off the coast of Cape Elizabeth, Maine, at 12:14 PM on Monday 23 April 1945 with the loss of 49 of her Officers and crewmen (courtesy of the author).

The U.S. Coast Guard manned U.S.S. *Nantucket* (formerly the Nantucket lightship *LV-112*), in her wartime configuration, armed, painted Navy gray (rather than red), with light and radar beacons removed, and portholes blocked off, as she took on the role as the Portland Gate Examination Vessel. Having been only two miles away when the *PE-56* exploded, she took part in the rescue of the *PE-56* survivors in the minutes following the sinking (courtesy of Arthur Gay).

The distinctive conning tower insignia of the German Type IXC/40 U-boat *U-853* with a red, trotting horse on a yellow shield and the U-boat's number, below. The "red and yellow markings" were witnessed by at least one of the *PE-56* survivors and was later confirmed by U.S. Navy hard-hat diver Edwin Bockelman when he descended to inspect the wreck of the sunken U-boat on 6 May 1945 (courtesy of Harry Cooper of Sharkhunters International).

The U.S. Navy Destroyer U.S.S. *Selfridge* (*DD-357*) approaching the Grand Trunk Pier in Portland, Maine, to deliver the survivors and bodies of the men recovered from the sinking of the *PE-56* in the early afternoon hours on Monday 23 April 1945 (courtesy of Clifford Chambers).

Officers and crewmen of the U.S. Navy destroyer U.S.S. *Selfridge* (DD-357), assisting in the transfer of the *PE-56* casualties from the *Selfridge* to the Grand Trunk Pier Naval Dispensary at Portland, Maine, on 23 April 1945 (courtesy of Clifford Chambers).

The 368 foot, 5,353 ton, C.H. Sprague & Son Steamship Company collier S.S. *Black Point*, the last American flagged merchant ship sunk by a German U-boat during WWII. She was torpedoed and sunk by the *U-853* at 5:35 PM on 5 May 1945 off Point Judith, Rhode Island, with the loss of 11 merchant crewmen and one U.S. Navy armed guard (courtesy of the Sprague Steamship Company).

An aerial photograph taken by a U.S. Navy ZNP Type blimp (*K-16* or *K-58*) as the U.S. Navy destroyer escort U.S.S. *Atherton* (*DE-169*) delivers a depth-charge attack on the German U-boat *U-853* East of Block Island, Rhode Island, on the morning of 6 May 1945 (courtesy of Duane Tollaksen).

Officer and crewmen aboard the Coast Guard manned Tacoma-Class Patrol Frigate U.S.S. *Moberly* (*PF-63*), examining debris that surfaced following the sinking of the German U-boat *U-853*, including Commander Frömsdorf's cap (courtesy of John McDonald).

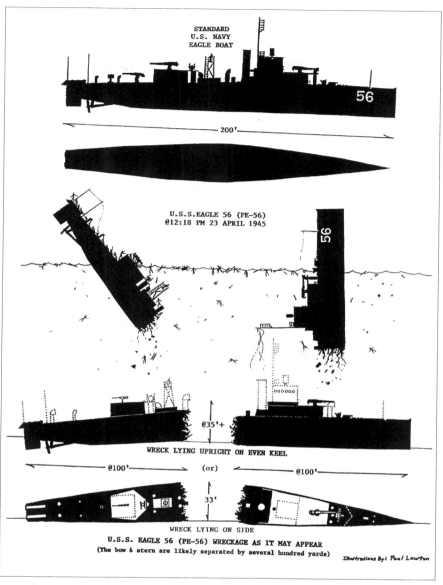

STANDARD
U.S. NAVY
EAGLE BOAT

56

— 200' —

U.S.S. EAGLE 56 (PE–56)
@12:18 PM 23 APRIL 1945

56

@35'+

WRECK LYING UPRIGHT ON EVEN KEEL

— @100' — (or) — @100' —

33'

WRECK LYING ON SIDE

U.S.S. EAGLE 56 (PE–56) WRECKAGE AS IT MAY APPEAR
(The bow & stern are likely separated by several hundred yards)

Illustrations By: Paul Lawton

Author Paul Lawton's illustration of an Eagle Class sub chaser, showing how she sank as described by her surviving Officer and crewmen, and how she might appear on the bottom, as a training aid for the *Eagle 56* Deep Dive Team, to assist them in their forensic investigation of the wreck in order to attempt to determine the nature and origin of the explosion that sank her (courtesy of the author).

World-renowned side-scan sonar expert, Garry Kozak (left), diver and Maine Maritime Historian, Chris Hugo, and the author, Paul Lawton (right), looking over side-scan sonar data aboard the search and survey vessel *Salvage One*, while searching Casco Bay for the wreck of the *PE-56* in July of 2000.

The author, Paul Lawton, wreck diving with fellow *PE-56* Search Team member Chris Hugo in the Gulf of Maine in 2002. Behind him on the right is an enormous Scotch Type fire-tube marine (ships) boiler, not the type that was installed aboard the *PE-56* (photo taken by Chris Hugo).

The author, Paul Lawton (center), with Mary Alice (Heyd) Hultgren, formerly a Naval Reserve member of the WAVES (Women Accepted for Volunteer Emergency Service), a Legal Yeoman and stenographer who took statements from the *PE-56* survivors following the sinking. They are with survivor, John Breeze, at the New England School of Law in Boston on 5 October 1998, where the author took their statements under oath about their recollections of those events (courtesy of the author).

Westerlund Kiddies Miss Dad on Victory Day

V-E DAY is small consolation for Mrs. Ivar Westerlund, Jr., 164 Belair street, whose husband was an-   seven; Paul, twe; Frederick, five, and Carol, nine. From details she has learned of the tragedy, Mrs. Westerlund does not believe her husband can be

The Westerlund family of Brockton, whose husband and father, S2c Ivar A. Westerlund, was lost aboard the *PE-56*, in a *Brockton Daily Enterprise* photo on or about 9 May 1945 (top), showing Ivar's widow, Phyllis and their children: Bob (7); Paul (2); Fred (5); and Carol (9). Below that, the recreated Westerlund family photo taken in 2002 (courtesy of the Westerlund family).

(Seated left to right) Archivist and Curator of the U.S. Navy
Shipbuilding Museum aboard the U.S.S. *Salem*, the late Jim
Fahey, Senior Archivist at the U.S. Naval Historical Center at the
Washington Navy Yard, the late Bernard Cavalcante, the author's
father, the late Judge (Ret.) James Lawton, Diver and Maine
Maritime historian, Chris Hugo, U.S. Navy Captain William Glass
(Ret.), and other Navy and Coast Guard dignitaries aboard the
U.S.S. *Salem* at the Purple Heart Awards Ceremony on 8 June
2002 (courtesy of Luke Sweeney).

The members of the "U.S.S. *Eagle 56* (*PE-56*) Search Team" aboard the search and survey vessel *Salvage One* out of the Merri-Mar Yacht Basin on the Merrimack River, Newburyport, Massachusetts. The Search Team members included (left to right) Tom Mackie of Trimble Navigation, Inc., Garry Kozak of Klein Associates (side-scan sonar), Inc., Fred Westerlund, Captain Jay Lesinsky, Paul Westerlund, Robert Westerlund, the author, Paul Lawton, Chris Hugo and Scott Uhlman. The Team is shown during their 12 to 14 July 2000 search for the wreck of the *PE-56* off the coast of Portland, Maine (courtesy of the author).

The author, Paul Lawton (left), with *PE-56* survivors John Scagnelli, Harold Petersen and John Breeze, aboard the U.S.S. *Salem* (*CA-139*) in Quincy, Massachusetts on 8 June 2002, for the Purple Heart Awards Ceremony. Secretary of the Navy (SECNAV) Gordon England signed the official Correction of the Navy's record on 26 June 2001, changing the cause of the sinking of the *PE-56* from an accidental "boiler Explosion" to "enemy action" (torpedo attack) by the *U-853*. By that unprecedented action, fifty-one men became eligible to receive the Purple Heart Medal, 49 posthumously (courtesy of Luke Sweeney).

The bronze and granite memorial marker to the Officers and crewmen of the U.S.S. *Eagle* (*PE-56*) at Fort Williams State Park in Cape Elizabeth, Maine, that was dedicated on the 60th Anniversary of the sinking on 23 April 2005. It was paid for with private funds raised by the families and friends of the *PE-56* Officers and crew, and stands on the cliff walk approximately 290 feet Southwest of the Portland Head Lighthouse (courtesy of the author).

Acknowledgments

We are indebted to many people for their kind and generous assistance in researching and documenting the loss of the U.S.S. *Eagle 56* (*PE-56*), the advancement of our effort to get posthumous recognition for the Officers and crewmen killed and wounded aboard the *PE-56*, and the correction of this chapter in naval history. In particular, I would like to thank:

Senior Archivist at the Naval Historical Center in Washington, DC, the late Bernard Cavalcante

Barry Zerby, of the Modern Military Records: Textual Archives Division of the National Archives at College Park, Maryland

The late Jim Fahey, former Archivist and Curator aboard the U.S. Navy Shipbuilding Museum, U.S.S. *Salem* (*CA-139*), at Quincy, Massachusetts

Diver, marine biologist, shipwreck researcher & illustrator, Chris Hugo

Captains Jay & Wally Lesynski of the search vessel *Salvage I*

Curator, Horst Bredow, Jak P. Mallmann Showell and Horst Schwenk at the U-Boot-Archiv at Cuxhaven-Altenbruch, Germany

Naval historian and author, Prof. Dr. Jurgen Rohwer of Weinstadt, Germany

Duane M. Tollaksen (USN Ret.)

Cathleen Latendresse at the Henry Ford Museum, Dearborn, Michigan

Ann Hasinger & Dawn Stitzel of the History, Reference and Preservation Division at the United States Naval Institute, Annapolis, Maryland

The Honorable Andrew H. Card, Jr. Chief of Staff to President
    George W. Bush

Dr. William S. Dudley, Director of Naval History and Captain
    Marshall A. Hall, former Deputy Director of Naval History at
    the U.S. Naval Historical Center in Washington, DC

Chief of Naval Operations (CNO) Admiral Vernon E. Clark

Secretary of the Navy (SECNAV) Gordon R. England

General Mark Rosenkerr, Deputy Assistant to the President and
    Director of the White House Military Office

Christopher J. Rouin, Director of the White House Military Affairs
    Office, and Lieutenant Scott Boris, White House Liaison to
    the Office of the Secretary of the Navy

Susan Abbott, of the National Archives and Records
    Administration, Old Military and Civilian Records Textual
    Archives Service Division at Washington, DC

PE-56 survivors: the late John Breeze, the late Harold Petersen and
    the late John P. Scagnelli

Legal Yeoman at the U.S. Navy Court of Inquiry on the sinking of
    the *PE-56*, the late Mary Alice (Heyd) Hultgren

Court stenographer, John Mahaney

The family of Ivar A. Westerlund (lost aboard the *PE-56*),
    including, but not limited to his widow, the late Phyllis
    (Kendrick), and children: Fred, Bob, Paul and the late Carol
    (Cushwa)

Sister and brother-in-law of Harold R. Rodman (lost aboard the
    PE-56), Elaine & Vincent Mitchell

Former Officers and crewmen aboard the U.S.S. *Selfridge* (*DD-357*),
    including, but not limited to the late: Roger Fisher, Jr., Joseph
    Breen, Brace Bennitt, Jr., Clifford Chambers, Robert Ferree,
    Edwin Walker and Thomas Welch

Former Officer aboard the U.S.S. *Woolsey* (*DD-437*), the late
    Lieutenant, Robert Cohen

Former crewman aboard the U.S.S. *Nantucket* (*LV-112*), the late
    Arthur Gay
Former Sonarman 2nd Class aboard the U.S.C.G.C. *Moberly*
    (*PF-63*), the late Richard DuBurg
Former crewman aboard the *PT-314*, the late Thomas Houston
The late William Heckendorf, former combat air-crewman aboard
    a PBY5A "Catalina" of patrol squadron VPB-92 out of the
    Quonset Point (RI) Naval Air station
The late Oliver Littleton, former Commander (Ensign) of the
    coastal minesweeper U.S.S. *Acme* (*AMc-61*)
Widow of *PE-56* survivor, the late Mrs. John (Lorraine) Luttrell
Divers, authors & maritime historians: Professor Henry Keatts, and
    Gary Gentile
Internationally renowned side-scan sonar expert Garry Kozak of
    Klein Associates, Inc. of Salem, New Hampshire
Tom Mackie of Trimble Navigation Limited
The late Glen Reem of Dolphin Diving & Underwater Exploration
LCdr John Gordon Bradley, Jr. formerly of composite squadron
    VC-15
Military researcher Scott Stets
Maine lighthouse and coast defense fortification researcher and
    author, Stephen Lyons
Professor Joel Eastman of the University of Southern Maine
Commander, Edward J. Melanson, Jr. (U.S.N.) of Springfield,
    Virginia
Commander, C. Roger Wallin U.S.N.R. (Ret.) Combat Systems
    Department: U.S. Naval Undersea Warfare Center, Newport,
    Rhode Island
Engineer & diver, Peter Kerrebrock, of Draper Labs, Inc. (formerly
    with the U.S.N. Undersea Warfare Center at Newport, Rhode
    Island)
U.S.C.G. Commander, Liam Slein, Marine Safety Center,
    Washington, DC

Naval/marine architect & forensic engineer, the late William
    Garzke, Jr., of Gibbs & Cox, Inc.
Delaware College History Professor and Curator of the Fort Miles
    Historical Association, Dr. Gary Wray
David Guaraldi, Senior New Technology Specialist at Cognex Corp.
    of Natick, Massachusetts
Harry Cooper, President of Sharkhunters International, Hernando,
    Florida
Gudmundur Helgason of the U-Boat Net, Hafnarfjordur, Iceland
German/English translator, the late Dr. Chester Claff
Proofreader, Grace Peirce
Archivist, Archives II Reference Section (DT2) at the National
    Archives at College Park, Maryland, Nathaniel Patch
Photographer, the late Stanley Bauman
The late Congressman, John Joseph "Joe" Moakley (1927-2001)
The Nomad [Deep Dive] Team members: Ryan King, Jeff
    Goudreau, Bob Foster, Danny Allan, Mark Bowers, Don
    Ferrara, Nate Garrett, and Josh Cummings
To my late parents, Jim (10/20/25-03/20/07) and Jeanne
    (10/09/27-11/25/10) Lawton
And to all of our families and friends.

Appendix I

U.S.S. *Eagle 56* (*PE-56*): U.S. Navy Casualties & Survivors
23 April 1945

PE-56 OFFICERS & ENLISTED MEN KILLED

(Officers: Bodies Not Recovered)

Lt. James G. Early (Commander), U.S.N.R.

Lt. (jg) John R. Laubach, U.S.N.R.

Lt. (jg) Ambrose G. Vanderheiden, U.S.N.R.

Ens. Seth E. Chapin, U.S.N.R.

Ens. Roy F. Swan, U.S.N.R.

(Enlisted Men: Bodies Not Recovered)

John Joseph Alexander, F2C, U.S.N.R.

James Orval Brown, CGM, U.S.N.

Robert Gurnett Coleman, SC3C, U.S.N.R.

Percy Collins, StM2C, U.S.N.R.

James Oliver Cunningham, S1C, U.S.N.R.

Robert Lee Davies, SoM2C, U.S.N.R.

Joseph Patrick Gegan, CM3C, U.S.N.R.

Harold Samuel Glenn, MM1C, U.S.N.R.

Walter Wrenn Goe, MM2C, U.S.N.R.

John Rodrigues Gonzales, WT2C, U.S.N.R.

Arthur Albert Grosch, Cox, U.S.N.R.

William Lloyd Harden, CPhM, U.S.N.R.

James Paul Johnson, PhM1C, U.S.N.

Norris Wilbur Jones, F1C, U.S.N.R.

Robert Velgene Kessler, S2C, U.S.N.R.

Joseph Andrew Lydon, RM2C, U.S.N.R.

Maurice Joseph Manning, WT3C, U.S.N.R.

Edwin Frederick Mathys, CMM U.S.N.

Joseph Howard McKenzie, MM3C, U.S.N.R.

John Charles Merk, EM2C, U.S.N.R.

Frederick Michelsen, MM1C, U.S.N.R.

Willie B. Morgan, CBM, U.S.N.

Zug Chesley Phelps, SM1C, U.S.N.R.

Christopher Columbus Phillips, StM3C, U.S.N.R.

Jasper Davis Pulley, S1C, U.S.N.

Virgil Quinn, Jr. SC2C, U.S.N.R.

Harold Ralph Rodman, Y1C, U.S.N.R.

Achibald Ronald, S2C, U.S.N.R.

George Sabatino, S2C, U.S.N.R.

Edwin Joseph Schneider, RM3C, U.S.N.R.

Joseph Frederick Setzer, RM2C, U.S.N.R.

Eliott Massey Shinn, QM2C, U.S.N.R.

James Hutchnes Smith, StM2C, U.S.N.R.

Nathan Cheney Stafford, F1C, U.S.N.R.

Leonard Jozef Surowiec, F1C, U.S.N.R.

James Francis Talley, S2C, U.S.N.R.

Raymond Robert Wallace, S2C, U.S.N.R.

Henry Louis Wengert, S2C, U.S.N.R.

Ivar Adolph Westerlund, S2C, U.S.N.R.

Ellis Elmer Whitcomb, S2C, U.S.N.R.

Ralph William Woods, MM2C, U.S.N.R.

Earle E. Young, MM2C, U.S.N.R.

(Enlisted Men: Bodies Recovered)

Paul Jaron Knapp, S2C, U.S.N.R.

George William Neugen, MM1C, U.S.N.R.

PE-56 SURVIVING OFFICER & ENLISTED MEN

(Officer)

Lt. (jg) John P. Scagnelli (Engineer), U.S.N.R.

(Enlisted Men)

John L. Breeze, MM2C, U.S.N.R.

Oscar F. Davis, MM3C, U.S.N.R.

Lawrence L. Edwards, GM3C, U.S.N.R.

Cletus J. Frane, MM3C, U.S.N.R.

John A. Happoldt, S2C, U.S.N.R.

Daniel E. Jaronik, S1C, U.S.N.R.

Edward G. Lockhart, MM1C, U.S.N.R.

John E. Luttrell, S1C, U.S.N.R.

Harold H. Petersen, MM1C, U.S.N.R.

Joseph C. Priestas, WT2C, U.S.N.R.

William A. Thompson, F1C, U.S.N.R.

John A. Wisniewski, RdM3C, U.S.N.R.

Five Officers & 44 Enlisted Men (49 Total) Killed, Two Bodies (Enlisted Men) Recovered (47 Lost), 1 Officer & Twelve Enlisted Men Rescued (62 Total Complement).

Appendix II

World War II Era German Torpedoes

The standard World War II era German torpedo, or "eel" was 21 inches (53.3 centimeters) in diameter, approximately 23.5 feet (7.16 meters) long, weighed as much as 3,528 pounds, and contained a (274kg) 604 pound type KE1 warhead (T-5), or (280kg) 617 pound warhead (G7s), containing an explosive mixture similar in composition to the American explosive called Torpex, consisting of cyclonite (RDX), TNT and aluminum flakes (early models contained gun-cotton 36). These torpedoes were capable of varying speeds and ranges, depending on the model, from 5,000 meters at 44 knots; 7,500 meters at 40 knots; 12,500 meters at 30 knots (G7a), or 5,750 meters at 24.5 knots (T-5). Torpedoes such as the G7a had variable range and speed settings, and the performance of electric powered torpedoes varied depending on whether the attack scenario provided sufficient time to pre-heat the torpedo's batteries, significantly increasing their performance prior to launch.

Early model torpedoes such as the Type G7a or (T-1) were propelled by compressed gas/internal-combustion motors which left behind a conspicuous wake of bubbles, often giving the target vessel time to locate the threat and take evasive action. Later models such as the Type G7e or (T-2) and the Type V or (T-5), however, were propelled by an electric motor powered by a 36 cell (T-5), or 52 cell (G7e) lead-acid storage battery, allowing them to run almost invisibly as they closed on their targets.

Early model torpedoes were detonated by an inertial percussion or contact/impact fuse (Aufschlagzundung) or AZ (Pi 4c) fuse, which exploded the warhead upon impact with the ship's hull. Many of these torpedoes proved faulty, however, either failing to detonate on contact, or failing to run at the proper depth setting, usually too deep, allowing them to pass harmlessly below the target ship's hull without exploding. Models such as the standard unguided "magnetic" Type G7a (T-1) and G7e (T-2) series, and the advanced passive-acoustic homing Type Vs incorporated a redundant magnetic proximity (Magnetzundung-Pistole) or Mz-Pi (TZ 5) detonator pistol (ignitor), designed to detonate the warhead after entering, then beginning to break away from the target ship's strongest magnetic field. This made the torpedo's depth setting less critical, often exploding below the ship's hull, lifting her out of the water and breaking her keel with catastrophic results.

Other advanced models included the "Federapparat" torpedo (FaT), or so-called "spring-loaded" torpedo, which ran on a set course for a fixed distance before switching to a zigzag pattern, increasing its chances of striking a ship steaming in close convoy formation, and the "Lagen unabhangiger" torpedo (LuT), which operated much like the FaT, but had longer range and a more powerful warhead than earlier Type G7 series torpedoes.

The Type V (T-5) also designated the G7es "Zaunkonig" (wren) passive-acoustic homing torpedo (called "GNAT" by the Allies, an acronym for German Navy Acoustic Torpedo), employed 16 direction finding, passive-acoustic receivers (transducers), amplifiers attached to a guidance system and a series of electronic servo-motor operated steering vanes on the rudder and hydroplane controls which would allow it to home onto the loudest part of the target ship, usually toward her engine room, shaft alleys, or propellers, destroying vital machinery such as her engines, drive reduction gears, rudders and props.

Most torpedoes were fitted with an arming safety device in the form of a small propeller fitted at the nose of the warhead. Upon launch from the torpedo tube, hydrodynamic forces unscrewed the propeller from the detonating cap after traveling a safe distance from the submarine. In doing so, the detonator's firing hammer was freed, arming the torpedo's inertial and magnetic detonator pistols.

Because the nose of the Type V (T-5) torpedo contained the acoustic array, however, the propeller-type arming safety device was replaced by a small water-wheel device, which was recessed in the side of the torpedo. By the end of World War II Germany had begun the development of a revolutionary new type of torpedo designated the Type XI (T-11). Very little information is available about the latest German acoustic torpedoes, as few actually fell into the hands of the Allies after the war. One source indicated that the T-11s employed active-acoustic homing capabilities, allowing the T-11 to actually transmit an acoustic "ping" which reflected off the intended target, back to the torpedo's acoustic array, where it could home-in on the target ship. Other sources, however indicate that the T-11 was merely a more advanced model than the T-5, allowing it to differentiate between certain acoustic signatures, and to target the high-pitched sound of a destroyer's turbines, rather than the more mechanical sounds of reciprocating steam engines found on most merchant ships of the time. It is believed that as many as three dozen T-11s were manufactured before Germany's surrender, though there is no record that any were actually used in combat.

All of these torpedoes required constant and meticulous maintenance and recharging of their batteries, depth setting apparatus, guidance system, gyroscope calibration, and lubrication, keeping the torpedo room "mixers" or torpedo handlers, busy around the clock.

German World War II era torpedoes were expensive, complicated to manufacture and contained considerable amounts of strategic materials. The early type G7a, for example, contained as much as 816 pounds (370kg) of copper, took up to 3,730 man-hours to fabricate, and cost as much as 24,000 Reichsmarks. During World War II the German Navy "Kriegsmarine" launched more than 38,000 torpedoes.

Appendix III

Why Did the *U-853* Surface after Sinking the *PE-56* & S.S. *Black Point*?

The *U-853* may have momentarily surfaced after executing the submerged torpedo attacks on the *Eagle 56* and the S.S. *Black Point* because of the U-boat's failure to maintain proper trim control after launching her torpedo(es). In order for a U-boat to maintain proper "trim" (the control of a submerged submarine's depth and equilibrium), the crew had to regularly track the boat's displacement (weight), throughout her patrol, including daily measurements of fuel, food and fresh water consumption, and the discharge of ordnance (torpedoes, mines, artillery and anti-aircraft munitions), garbage, and human waste.

Minor changes to a boat's trim such as those caused by movement of fuel, personnel, stores and equipment, as well as currents and other hydrodynamic forces, could usually be compensated for by adjustment of the bow and stern hydroplanes. Rapid and extreme changes in the boat's buoyancy and trim, however, such as that resulting from a submerged torpedo launch, required excellent training, experience and discipline in order to keep the boat from broaching the surface, potentially exposing herself in a vulnerable position, and compromising some of the tactical advantage obtained from a submerged attack.

The immediate loss of displacement a U-boat experienced upon launching her torpedoes (1,600 kilograms per torpedo), required simultaneous action by certain crewmen to quickly flood the appropriate trim tanks and regulator cells with sufficient sea water to counterbalance the rapid increase in buoyancy, and maintain proper depth. This procedure required strict coordination with the "planesmen" (controlling the hydroplanes), and anything short of perfect execution could cause the boat to sink below periscope depth, or rise uncontrollably and broach the surface.

This phenomenon was not uncommon with inexperienced U-boat Officers and crewmen, particularly those lacking sufficient experience in the firing of live, or practice torpedoes. This shortcoming increased toward the end of the war, and may have been the reason the *U-853* momentarily surfaced after Commander Frömsdorf fired either a single passive-acoustic homing Type V (T-5), or "Facherschuss," simultaneous spread, or fan launch of two or more unguided Type G7e torpedoes at the U.S.S. *Eagle 56*.

Other possible explanations why the *U-853* momentarily surfaced after these submerged torpedo attacks on the *PE-56* and the S.S. *Black Point*, may have included intentional, though highly dangerous acts of defiant bravado by the young Commander, Frömsdorf, or his desire to get a better view of the destruction he inflicted for the purpose of battle damage assessment (BDA) (Commander, C. Roger Wallin (U.S.N.R. Ret). A more perplexing question that may never be answered is: What were Commander Frömsdorf's mysterious intentions in having his crew attempt to launch an inflatable life raft after sinking the S.S. *Black Point*?

Appendix IV

S.S. *Black Point*: Merchant Crewmen & U.S. Navy Armed Guards

Casualties and Survivors

5 May 1945

U.S. Navy Armed Guard Killed

Lonnie Lloyd Whitson, BM2C, U.S.N., Youngsville, NC

U.S. Navy Armed Guard Survivors

Harry T. Berryhill, S1C, U.S.N.

Alcester R. Colella, S1C, U.S.N., Malden, MA

Stephen Svetz, S1C, U.S.N.

Gustav A. Vogelbacher, SM1C, U.S.N., New York

Merchant Crewmen Killed

William Antilley, Abilene, TX

Geo P. Balser, Queens, NY

Leo H. Beck, St.Louis, MO

Laurel F. Clark, Brinkman, OK

Cleo Hand, Hazelhurst, GA

Robert L. Korb, Newport News, VA

Reino Lindstrom, Finland

Milton Matthews, St. Louis, MO

Marvin A. Mertinek, Warda, TX

Ansey L. Morgan, Virginia

Richard C. Shepson, Boundbrook, NJ

Captain & Merchant Crewmen Survivors

Master: Captain Charles E. Prior, Belfast, ME

Clair V. Berry, 1st Mate, Cape Elizabeth, ME

Calvin Baumgartner, Baltimore, MD

Earl Campbell, Hyde Park, MA

Francis E. Curran, Mess Boy, Waltham, MA

James Davis, Gloucester, VA

Joseph R. Desourdy, Mess Boy, Southbridge, MA

Lawrence Drayton, Chief Cook, South Dartmouth, MA

Argvris P. Economou, Bronx, NY (Greece)

James C. Fowlkes, Milton, NC

Abel Gomes, Utility Man, Providence, RI (Portugal)

Francis L. Kelley, Chief Engineer, Chelsea, MA

Joseph W. Kelley, 2nd Cook, Somerville, MA

James N. Lane, 2nd Engineer, Concord, MA

Patrick N. Leary, Watertender, Watertown, MA

Howard A. Locke, Raynolds, GA

Thomas P. Mello, 1st Engineer, Taunton, MA

Rufus K. Nash, Newport News, VA

Sanfred Navma (or Sanford Nauha?), Fireman, (YMCA)
Brockton, MA (Finland)

Rivard Nehls, Watertown, WI

Gordon Nelson, Minnesota

L. Roland Pelletier, Purser, Unity, ME

Joseph S. Pires (or Piers ?), Chief Steward, South Dartmouth, MA

Marcus L. Rowe, Portsmouth, VA

Glennen W. Ryan, Portage Des Souix, MO

John E. Shoaff, Jr., Beaver Falls, PA

Homer P. Small, 3rd Mate, East Machias, ME

John N. Smith, Messick, VA

Joseph R. Tharl, Radio Operator, Franklin, MA

Stewart M. Whitehouse, Arlington, MA

Appendix V

U-853: German Navy Officers & Crewmen (55) Killed
5 & 6 May 1945

U-Boot-Archiv: Ehrentafel der Gefallenen (Honor-Role of Those Killed): *U-853*

(Rank/Rate; Name: first/last; DOB: day/month/year)

Lt. Hans-Ulrich Abele 11.03.23

MtrOGfr. Eugen Bartsch 31.07.25

MtrOGfr. Arthur Bereskin 22.01.23

MechGfr. Egon Bohm 22.08.23

MaschOGfr. Siegfried Brdlik 31.08.24

MechOGfr. Hermann Buhler 28.03.25

MaschOGfr. Anton Corbach 28.07.25

MtrOGfr. Paul Dorwald 18.10.24

MaschOGfr. Herbert Edler 21.08.24

OMasch. Helmut Fehrs 27.08.15

OLt. Helmut Frömsdorf 26.03.21

MtrOGfr. Oskar Gari 21.05.20

MaschOGfr. Heinz Geisler 22.11.19

SanMt. Werner Grahl 26.08.22

OMaschMt. Rudolf Greiner 27.01.22

MechMt. Kurt Heiligtag 06.03.20

FkOGfr. Rudolf Herbert 30.08.25

MaschMt. Herbert Holzer 19.04.24

MtrOgfr. Herbert Hoffmann 04.09.22

OStrm. Heinrich Kistner 13.08.20

MaschOGfr. Joseph Klein 14.03.25

MtrOGfr. Rudolf Lehmann 13.07.21

MaschMt. Willibald Liebscher 30.05.20

MaschOGfr. Gunter Luckei 27.05.25

BtsMt. Johann Lyhs 07.01.22

MaschOGfr. Erich Mazallik 25.03.24

MaschMt. Helmut Meier 29.03.23

OMaschMt. Willi Maker 31.01.23

MtrGfr. Helmut Mieschliwietz 08.09.26

MtrOGfr. Helmut Mruck 04.01.24

MaschOGfr. Franz Nasse 15.08.24

MaschGfr. Walter Pokel (*Keine Personalangaben*)

OLt. Gotthart Poorten 19.12.21

MechOGfr. Franz Porstner 24.05.24

FkGfr. Rgon Rauch 11.05.25

MaschOGfr. Berthold Reister 12.12.24

MaschOGfr. Heinrich Roseman 17.12.22

MtrGfr. Helmut Rosenmuller 25.03.26

OFkMstr. Erich Schaadt 03.05.16

FkOGfr. Lothar Schanz 15.05.24

Lt. Wolfgang Schancke 22.04.23

StrmMt. Kurt Schmidt 07.02.23

MechOGfr. Werner Schumann 06.09.24

MaschOGfr. Helmut Schwarz 26.06.24

BtsMt. Theo Schwenk 17.10.20

MtrOGfr. Herbert Suchy 15.11.22

MtrGfr. Alfred Trotz 21.04.26

MaschOGfr. Freidrich Volk 12.06.24

Lt. (Ing) Christian Wilde 04.05.19

MaschMt. Herbert Winkler 22.03.22

OMasch. Nicolaus Wolf 10.09.18

OMaschMt. Karl Wust 09.03.22

OMaschOGfr. Willibald Wulle 27.08.23

FkMt. Karl Wurster 06.12.23

MtrGfr. Karl-Heinz Zacher 05.11.26

Appendix VI

W.W.II Era Allied Anti-Submarine Detection Equipment, Countermeasures & Weapons Detection Equipment

ASDIC: British name for SONAR (Sounding Navigation And Ranging) underwater acoustic detection of objects via passive or active modes. Passive sonar allowed detection of the ambient noise generated by a submerged submarine, her motors and screws. When a stalked submarine dove and shut down its machinery and attempted to go "silent" however, "active" sonar was employed by the acoustic targeting "ping" that reflected off solid objects, revealing the U-boats' presence to the sonar operator's hydrophones. Some U.S. Navy blimps also employed "dunking-sonar" lowered into the water by low-flying airships to detect ambient noise generated by submerged U-boats. The acronym ASDIC, was derived from "Allied Submarine Detection Investigation Committee," the group initially in charge of its development.

Coastal Observation Towers: Usually rather simple, elevated, steel reinforced concrete block structures, they were constructed by the hundreds, if not thousands along Allied coastlines. Visual observation of suspicious activity was quickly radioed to nearby air and sea forces to investigate, and attack if necessary.

"Huff-Duff": (H/F-D/F or HF/DF) high-frequency direction-finding detection equipment, used to detect the bearing of German U-boat radio transmissions, from land, sea and airborne detection units. With multiple fixes on a single transmission, triangulation allowed for relatively precise location of the area from which the U-boat made the transmission. One German countermeasure against HF/DF was "Kurier" (Courier), a burst-transmitter that sent out an encrypted message in just a few seconds, reducing the time required for HF/DF receivers to obtain a good "cut" on the transmitting U-boat's signal, and making it more difficult to triangulate a fix on the target.

Leigh-Light: Powerful 80 million candlepower spotlight fitted to bottom of Royal Air Force (RAF) Coastal Command British-built Armstrong-Whitworth "Wellington" bombers, and a few other types of Allied aircraft, to illuminate surfaced U-boats at night, usually after being targeted by airborne radar. The Leigh-Light was only activated at a range of less than a mile from the U-boat while the aircraft made its attack run, so as to deny the sub sufficient time to dive, or man her anti-aircraft guns. The American version of the British Leigh-Light was known as the L7.

MAD: Magnetic (Airborne) Anomaly Detection. Airborne magnetic detection equipment carried by Allied aircraft, particularly U.S. Navy blimps, capable of detecting the magnetic field generated by a submerged U-boat or shipwreck, often used in conjunction with Huff-Duff, radar, sonar and sonobuoys to detect and track the movements of submarines to coordinate an attack by aircraft or surface ships.

Magnetic Loops: Underwater magnetic detection cables laid on the ocean floor around major ports and naval bases to detect the magnetic field generated by the passage of ferrous metal vessels. Signals picked up by the land-based receiving stations at either end of the magnetic loop could detect shipping activity, and any unseen anomalies in the area could indicate the presence of an enemy submarine.

Radar: Air, sea and land-based systems such as the Mark III ASV centimeter-wavelength radar units could detect a radar signal reflected from the hull and conning tower of a surfaced submarine, and even its small snorkel-induct head (exposed while snorkeling submerged), from miles away. Often used by Allied aircraft in concert with HF/DF and Leigh-Light to first target a surfaced U-boat, then illuminate if for strafing, depth-charge, or Fido attack.

Sonar: see **ASDIC**

Sonobuoys: (Hydrophone-Sonobuoys) Air delivered disposable acoustic receivers and radio transmitters dropped in a square or circular pattern in areas of known U-boat activity. Upon hitting the water, sonobuoys deployed a passive acoustic receiver (hydrophone) at the end of a 21 foot cable and activated a wireless transmitter, relaying sonar range estimates of acoustic targets, back to ASW aircraft. Triangulation of bearing information transmitted from multiple sonobuoys provided a fix on the U-boat target allowing for depth-charge or Fido attack on the unseen enemy.

"**Ultra**": Allied (Initially British) monitoring and decryption of secret coded German radio transmissions including the latest 4-rotor "Enigma" code "Triton." "Ultra" decryption center sub-tracking room known as "Op20G," in Washington, DC, and Britain's Naval (decrypt) Section at Bletchley Park in Buckinghamshire, England constantly monitored encrypted German radio transmissions between U-boats and "Befehlshaber der Unterseeboote" (BdU), U-boat headquarters, gaining valuable operational and tracking information on German U-boats throughout the war.

COUNTERMEASURES

CAT Gear: (Canadian Anti-Acoustic Torpedo) Mechanical noisemakers streamed (towed) behind merchant vessels and warships, often as simple as clanging metal bars drawn by cable, intended as a countermeasure to confuse and misdirect German Type V (T-5) also designated the G7es "Zaunkonig" (wren) passive-acoustic homing torpedoes, to safely detonate a distance behind the targeted ship (see also: **Foxer**).

Coastal Black-Outs: In order to confuse and misdirect U-boats lurking off-shore, coastal areas enforced black-outs, darkening windows and lights near or facing the coastline. This was intended to prevent a lighted background for U-boat's to get a visual fix on transiting merchant vessels and Allied warships. This concept also involved the removal of many navigational markers, lightships and the darkening of lighthouses.

Convoys: Groups of armed and unarmed merchant tankers, freighters and troopships, sailing in protected formation and guarded by Allied escort warships (and often aircraft). With the staggering Allied and neutral merchant shipping losses incurred in the early years of the war, convoy routes were established between friendly ports to deliver millions of tons of strategic materials to Britain and Russia needed to stem the Axis advance.

"Foxer" (FXR): British streamed (towed) mechanical noisemaker similar to CAT Gear, designed as a countermeasure to confuse and misdirect German T-5 "GNAT" passive acoustic-homing torpedoes away from the intended target ship (see: **CAT Gear**).

Nets (anti-sub): Intricate steel mesh nets (also known as "booms') strung between buoys and floats, designed to prevent the penetration of U-boats into protected waters such as harbors, etc. Submarines could become entangled in the nets where they were vulnerable to attack by aircraft and surface vessels. Harbor defenses usually included a combination of anti-submarine nets, magnetic loops, moored nautical-mines; coastal observation towers and shore-gun batteries.

ANTI-SUBMARINE WEAPONS

Armed Merchant Ships: After the beginning of the war many pre-war merchant freighters and tankers were equipped with deck guns and anti-aircraft armaments, manned by U.S. Navy armed guards assigned to protect the ships from enemy attack. After America's entry in the war shipyards began turning out large numbers of specially built "Liberty" and "Victory" ships, and T-2 tankers, fitted with gun-tubs to accommodate a number of defensive gun configurations. These armaments did more to boost crew morale, than present a viable defense against submarine attack, however.

ASW Aircraft: Anti-Submarine Warfare aircraft flown Patrol Squadrons (VPs), by the U.S. Navy; U.S. Army Air Force (USAAF); Royal Air Force (RAF); and Royal Canadian Air Force (RCAF), a few of which included the: Flying-boats: PBY and PBY5A "Catalina"; Martin "Mariner"; British "Sunderland"; OS2U "Kingfisher" and the Canadian Canso "A." Bombers: Boeing B-17 "Flying Fortress"; Consolidated B-24 "Liberator"; British-built Hadley Page "Halifax"; Armstrong-Whitworth "Whitley" & "Wellington"; American-designed Lockheed "Hudsons" and PV Vega "Ventura." Fighters: antiquated British-built Fairy "Swordfish" bi-planes; Grumman F4F "Wildcat" and Grumman F6F "Hellcat." Torpedo-bombers: Grumman TBF & TBM "Avenger." Blimps: U.S. Navy ZNP "K" Type (252 feet in length and armed with Mark XVII depth-charges). Many were fitted with radar, some with Leigh-lights or sonobuoys, and almost all were capable of delivering heavy machine-gun and cannon fire, rockets, depth-charges, mines or torpedoes to German U-boats. ASW aircraft could also vector additional aircraft and surface vessels to the area to hunt the suspect U-boat.

CAM Ships: Catapult Armed Merchantmen (freighters) fitted with a single British Hawker Hurricane aircraft, catapult launched from the deck. The pilot usually had no alternative at the end of his flight but to ditch his aircraft near a friendly ship and parachute into the ocean, hoping to be picked up and rescued. These ships were also often referred to as Merchant Aircraft Catapult (MAC) ships.

Depth-Charges: Anti-submarine depth-bombs included the American-made 420 pound Mk 6 & 520 pound Mk 8; the British Mk VII, and the 325 pound Mk XVII "ashcan" types; and the 600 pound Mk 9 "Teardrop" type depth-charges. Depending on the amount of ballast contained in the charge (usually lead or concrete), certain types of depth-charges sank at different rates of speed, and could be fitted with either hydrostatic (depth-set), or magnetic detonating pistols. Hydrostatic pistols detonated the main explosive charge at a pre-set depth, while magnetic pistols only fired after entering the ferrous magnetic field of a submerged U-boat. The 520 pound Magnetic Mk 8 for example contained 250 pounds of explosives and 150 pounds of lead with a sink rate of 11.5 feet/second, and carried a hydrostatic back-up fuse to detonate if it did not fall close enough to a U-boat to detonate the magnetic pistol. Depth-charges could either be fired from the side of the attacking warship by "K-gun" and "Y-gun" spigot-launchers, or rolled off fixed, fantail mounted depth-charge racks.

Escort Carriers: (CVEs) Also known as "Jeep Carriers," small American made aircraft carriers, they were the core of individual anti-submarine "Hunter-Killer" groups. These Bogue Class and Casablanca Class aircraft carriers were smaller than full size fleet carriers, and carried between 25 and 30 fighters and torpedo-bomber type aircraft.

"Fido": American-made air-dropped Mark XXIV (Mk 24) "homing-mine" passive acoustic-homing torpedo, often delivered by Grumman TBF "Avenger" torpedo-bombers. Electrically powered, it was 19 inches in diameter and 7 feet long, with a 90 pound Torpex warhead. It was intended to be dropped from altitudes between 200 to 300 feet at speeds between 120 to 125 knots, with a submerged speed of 12 knots for a duration of between 10 to 15 minutes. Fido had a three-dimensional attack profile, and could dive to considerable depths, tracking and closing on the ambient noise of submarine's screws, where it was intended to detonate, usually with catastrophic results.

Guns: Surface ship and aircraft mounted guns varying in caliber from light British .303 and American .30 caliber machine-guns; to American .50 caliber Browning M2 heavy machine-guns; to automatic 20mm "Oerlikon" and 40mm "Bofors" anti-aircraft cannons; to heavier destroyer and destroyer escort deck-guns such as the 3-inch/50 caliber; 4-inch/50 cal.; & 5-inch/38 cal. Guns. Once a U-boat was depth-charged or otherwise forced to the surface, circling aircraft and warships would unleash a withering fusillade from all guns that could be brought to bear, to puncture the U-boat's thick pressure hull, and to kill crewmen attempting to man its deck-guns and flak cannon. Coastal defenses, particularly those around major harbors and naval bases were often protected by heavily fortified shore-gun batteries that were capable of engaging surfaced targets several miles out to sea.

"Hedgehog": Mk10 (and Mk 11) roll-stabilized Hedgehog projector was a heavy, surface ship mounted battery of 24 "ahead-throwing" 65 pound, electrically-fired, spigot launched, contact-fused depth-bombs, each containing 30 pound TNT or 35 pound Torpex warheads. Hedgehogs had a sink-rate of 21 feet per second, and with an average of 7.5 seconds in the air, they could reach a target down to 600 feet after only 35 seconds of "blind time." Hedgehogs could be fired up to 270 yards ahead of attacking warship in a circular (Mk 11) or elliptical (Mk 10) pattern, exploding on contact with the submarine. Employing a Monroe-effect shaped explosive charge, if contact was made with the U-boat's hull, it was almost always fatal. Soon after the end of W.W. II the Navy deployed the Mk 15 Hedgehog mount, which was not only roll (and pitch) stabilized, but also trainable.

Merchant Aircraft Catapult (MAC) Ships: (see: **CAM Ships**).

Minefields: Tethered nautical mines laid in areas around known U-boat operating areas, particularly around their bases and access routes to the open ocean such as the English Channel. Also used extensively around Allied anchorages, harbors and naval bases. Usually contact detonated, most harbor mine fields were command-detonated from fixed shore batteries employing magnetic loops and coastal observation towers to identify and track targets.

"**Mousetrap**": Mark 20 & Mk 22 Rocket-propelled 7.2 inch, 65 pound depth-bombs, each containing 31 pound TNT warheads. They were fired from a four-rail Mk 20 box-launcher (usually twin mounted with 8 rockets each), some were slightly trainable but not roll-stabilized, they were mounted at a fixed elevation of 48 degrees, on the fore-deck of a number of U.S. Navy patrol vessels. Much lighter, simpler and with a greater range than Hedgehog, several such box-launchers could be fitted on the bow of a destroyer, increasing lethality. The charges were fused for contact, and to counter-mine upon detonation of any one of the other charges striking the target. Mousetrap was a less effective alternative to Hedgehogs, but could be accommodated on smaller and lighter warships, where the much heavier Hedgehog projector mount, could not. Mousetrap also produced considerably less recoil that Hedgehog.

Q-Ships: Armed Allied warships disguised as harmless, small neutral merchant vessels. As in W.W.I they were intended to draw a hunting U-boat to the surface were it could sink the small ship with deck-gun fire, rather that expending a valuable torpedo. Once surfaced, concealed guns aboard the Q-Ship were to out-gun the U-boat. This ploy was well known to U-boat commanders after

W.W.I, and the W.W.II attempts to revive the old "trick" were not successful.

Retro-Bombs: Tube-launched, rocket-propelled 7.2 inch depth-bombs similar to Mousetrap rockets, carried by U.S. Navy ZNP Type blimps and intended for use in concert with MAD detection gear. Because MAD gear only gave an accurate position of submerged submarines when the blimp was directly overhead, conventional air-dropped weapons would land off target due to the forward velocity of the attacking airship. The retro-bomb delivered an accurate attack upon a submerged U-boat at the precise moment when the optimum MAD contact was made, as the attacking blimp was directly over the target.

Rockets: Air-to-surface solid-fuel rockets were made in several variants for use against surfaced and submerged U-boats. One version was a high-velocity three (3") inch diameter rocket weighing 66 pounds, carrying a 25 pound solid armor-piercing warhead. Fired from fighter aircraft from under-wing racks. Single fired or in salvo, they could penetrate a surfaced U-boat's conning tower or pressure hull. Another 7.2 inch rocket-propelled depth-bomb was carried by U.S. Navy ZNP Type blimps, and could be fired from altitude to attack U-boats submerged just below the surface, where the warhead would detonate on impact. After the war, anti-submarine testing was performed on a rocket-propelled depth-bomb resembling an enlarged Hedgehog, called Mk 108 (RUR-4) "weapon Alfa" (Able).

"Squid": British designed and introduced in 1943, three (3) barreled AS (anti-submarine) mortar Mk 4. Firing three 390 pound 12 inch diameter bomb shaped depth-charges (each containing 207 pound Minol II warheads), from surface ships in a triangular pattern, the charges were automatically fused by a fire-control computer at the last moment before firing to detonate at a specific depth, set by sonar. Squid had a sink-rate of 38 feet per second and could reach a target down to 600 feet after only 25 seconds. This weapon was considered to be slightly more effective than Hedgehog.

Surface Warships: A number of different types of surface warships were designed to hunt and kill enemy submarines. W.W.II era destroyers (DDs), destroyer-escorts (DEs), frigates, corvettes and sub-chasers were all outfitted to acoustically locate and track submarines by Huff-Duff, radar, and sonar (ASDIC); then to depth-charge, hedgehog, mousetrap or squid them to submerged destruction, or to force them to the surface where the submarine would be peppered in a fusillade of gun fire, and often rammed.

Bibliography

BOOKS

Blair, Clay. *Hitler's U-Boat War: The Hunted 1942-1945*. New York, NY: Random House, 1998.

Botting, Douglas. *The Seafarers: The U-Boats*. Alexandria, VA: Time-Life Books, 1979.

Browning, Robert M. Jr. *U.S. Merchant War Casualties of World War II*. Annapolis, MD: Naval Institute Press, 1996.

Busch, Rainer & Roll, Hans-Joachim. *German U-Boat Commanders of World War II: A Biographical Dictionary*. Annapolis, MD: Naval Institute Press, 1999.

Cahill, Robert Ellis. *New England's Strange Sea Sagas*. Peabody, MA: Chandler-Smith Publishing, 1984.

Chawning, Alpheus J. *The Approaching Storm: U-boats off the Virginia Coast During World War II*. Lively, VA: Brandylane Publishers, 1994.

Downie, Robert M. *Block Island: The Sea*. Block Island, RI: Book Nook Press, 1998.

Fahey, James C. *The Ships and Aircraft of the United States Fleet*, Second War Edition, New York, NY: Gemsco, Inc. 1944.

Fish, John P. *Unfinished Voyages*. Orleans, MA: Lower Cape Publishing, 1989.

Franklin, Bruce P. *The Buckley-Class Destroyer Escorts*. Annapolis, MD: Naval Institute Press, 1999.

Friedman, Norman. *U.S. Destroyers*. Annapolis, MD: Naval Institute Press, 1982.

Friedman, Norman. *U.S. Small Combatants*. Annapolis, MD: Naval Institute Press, 1987.

Gannon, Michael. *Operation Drumbeat*. New York, NY: Harper Collins Publishers, 1991.

Gentile, Gary. *Shipwrecks of Delaware and Maryland*. Philadelphia, PA: Gary Gentile Productions, 1990.

Gentile, Gary. *Track of the Gray Wolf: U-Boat Warfare on the U.S. Eastern Seaboard 1942-1945*. New York, NY: Avon Books, 1989.

Hadley, Michael L. *U-Boats Against Canada*. Montreal, Canada: McGill-Queen's University Press, 1985.

Hoyt, Edwin P. *U-Boats Offshore: When Hitler Struck America*. New York, NY: Stein and Day Publishers, 1978.

Jordan, Roger W. *The World's Merchant Fleets 1939*. Annapolis, MD: Naval Institute Press, 1999.

Keatts, Henry C., and Farr, George C. *Warships, Volume 1: Dive into History*. Houston, TX: Pisces Books. 1990.

Keatts, Henry C., and Farr, George C. *U-Boats, Volume 3: Diving Into History*. Houston, TX: Pisces Books, 1994.

Kemp, Paul. *U-Boats Destroyed: German Submarine Losses in the World Wars*. Annapolis, MD: Naval Institute Press, 1997.

Mallmann-Showell, Jak P. *U-Boats Under the Swastika*. Annapolis, MD: Naval Institute Press, 1987.

Miller, David. *U-Boats. An Illustrated History of the Raiders of the Deep*. Washington, DC: Pegasus Publishing, 2000.

Milner, Marc. *The U-Boat Hunters: The Royal Canadian Navy and the Offensive Against German Submarines*. Annapolis, MD: Naval Institute Press, 1994.

Niestle, Axel. *German U-Boat Losses During World War II: Details of Destruction*. Annapolis, MD: Naval Institute Press, 1998.

Rohwer, Jurgen. *Axis Submarine Successes. 1939-1945*. Annapolis, MD: Naval Institute Press, 1983.

Rohwer, Jurgen, and Hummelchen, Gerhard. *Chronology of War at Sea, 1939-1945: The Naval History of World War II*. Annapolis, MD: Naval Institute Press, 1992.

Roscoe, Theodore. *United States Destroyer Operations of World War II*. Annapolis, MD; Naval Institute Press, 1953.

Rossler, Eberhard. *The U-Boat: The Evolution and Technical History of German Submarines.* Annapolis, MD: Naval Institute Press, 1981.

Schroder, Walter K. *Defenses of Narragansett Bay in World War II.* Providence, RI: Providence Rhode Island Bicentennial Foundation, 1980.

Sheard, Bradley. *Lost Voyages: Two Centuries of Shipwrecks in the Approaches to New York.* Hong Kong: Aqua Quest Publications, 1998.

Wynn, Kenneth. *U-Boat Operations of the Second World War, Volume 1: Career Histories, U-1 to U-510.* Annapolis, MD: Naval Institute Press, 1997.

Wynn, Kenneth. *U-Boat Operations of the Second World War, Volume 2: Career Histories, U-511 to UIT25.* Annapolis, MD: Naval Institute Press, 1998.

Young, Peter, Brigadier. *The World Almanac of World War II.* New York, NY: Pharos Books, 1981.

OTHER PUBLISHED SOURCES

Associated Press. "Decades Later, Sinking is Tied to Enemy." August 30, 2001.

Boating World: Sound Edition. "The Last Battle of World War II Off Long Island," by Van R. Field. July 2004.

Boston Daily Record: "49 Die in Ship Blast 3 Miles off Maine." May 9, 1945.

Boston Globe: "Recent Attacks by U-Boats Kill 62 Off Atlantic Coast." May 10, 1945.

Boston Globe: "Captured U-Boat Crew in Boston." May 11, 1945.

Boston Globe: "Saga of Capt. Prior." June 6, 1945.

Boston Globe: "Survivor Recalls Attack Off R.I." May 8, 1995.

Boston Globe: "What Sank the Eagle?" March 12, 2000.

Boston Globe Magazine: "The Final Hours of the *U-853*." May 5, 1985.

Boston Herald: "Big-Bucks Compass Appraisal Doesn't Wreck His Day." May 26, 2006.

Boston Herald: "True Story About Sunken Subchaser Coming to Light." April 19, 2001.

Boston Herald: "Vindication Comes to Men of Sunken WWII Subchaser." August 26, 2001.

Brockton Enterprise: "Westerlund Kiddies Miss Dad on Victory Day." May 8, 1945.

Brockton Enterprise: "R.I. War Tragedy Rests 130 Feet Down." May 11, 1992.

Brockton Enterprise: "Dive Team Hopes to Solve a Mystery." May 30, 1999.

Brockton Enterprise: "Search at Sea." July 13, 2000.

Brockton Enterprise: "After 56 Years, Local Family Gets Military Justice." August 28, 2001.

Foster's Daily Democrat (Dover, NH) "U-boat Sunk Two-Days Before V-E Day: Barrington Man's Ship Helped Sink Sub Off R.I." May 3, 1995.

Daily Record (NJ): "WWII Survivor Lived to Tell Story, Morris Man Knew Truth About Eagle: Navy Finally Admits to Sinking by German Sub Off Maine Coast in 1945." September 9, 2001.

Dictionary of American Navy Fighting Ships, Volume VI. Naval History Division, Department of the Navy, Washington, DC: 1976.

Hendrickson, David H. *The Patrol Frigate Story: The Tacoma Class Frigates in World War II and Korean War 1943-1953*. The United States Coast Guard. 1999.

Herald Traveler: May 9, 1945.

Male magazine. "Mystery of the *U-853*: Million Dollar Treasure Off Rhode Island's Coast." July 1961.

New York Times: "49 Lost Off Maine In Navy Ship Blast." May 9, 1945.

New York Times: "U-Boat Sinks Destroyer off Cape May, All But 11 Lost." March 4, 1942.

New York Times: "14 Dead in 2 U-Boat Sinkings Off East Coast as V-E Nears." May 9?, 1945.

New York Times: "Recent Attacks by U-Boats Kill 62 Off Atlantic Coast." May 9, 1945.

New York Times: "56 Years Later, Navy Says German Sub Sank Ship Off Maine." September 4, 2001.

Portland Press Herald: "49 Die in Mysterious Boat Blast 3 Miles off Cape Elizabeth." May 9, 1945.

Portland Press Herald: "Survivors of Coast Guard Sinking in WW II Sought." April 24, 1995.

Portland Press Herald: "Obituary of John E. Luttrell, S1C, survivor of PE-56." September 24, 1996.

Portland Press Herald: "Sailor's family still feels slap 55 years later." November 12, 1999.

Portland Press Herald: "After 56 Years, The Truth Triumphs." August 29, 2001.

Rochester Democrat and Chronicle: "Truth Eases a Wartime Agony: Nazi Torpedo, Not Boiler Explosion, Sank Navy Ship." August 30, 2001.

Rochester Times Union: "Sailor Feared Dead; Area Man Survives Blast." May 9, 1945.

Rochester Journal: "Henrietta Man Escapes In Boat Blast Killing 49." May 9? 1945.

Ships' Data U.S. Naval Vessels, November 1, 1918. Government Printing Office, Washington, D.C. 1919.

The Advocate (Baton Rouge, LA). "New Evidence Shows German Submarine Sank U.S. Ship in 1945." August 30, 2001.

The Newport Daily News (Newport, RI). "Mystery Solved at Castle Hill: Discovery of Propellers Bring Closure for Brothers." Saturday and Sunday, June 26 and 27, 2004.

The News-Times (Danbury, CT): "Cause of the USS *Eagle*'s Sinking Was a U-boat, Not a Faulty Boiler." September 9, 2001.

United States Naval Institute Proceedings, "U-853—An End to the Story." Volume 87, Number 3, March 1961

United States Naval Institute Proceedings, Tollaksen, Ensign Duane M. "Last Chapter for *U-853*," December 1960.

United States Naval Institute Proceedings, Cianflone, Frank A. "The Eagle Boats of World War I," June 1973.

UNPUBLISHED SOURCES

Bureau of Ships: Construction and Repair, Statistics Division. Information Sheet No. 1., U.S.S. *Eagle 56*.

Ehrentafel der Gefallenen, Records & Photographs: *U-853*, U-Boot-Archiv. Cuxhaven-Altenbruch, Germany.

E-mails from military researcher Scott Richard Stets, M.Ed. "The Vet Detective" regarding LCDR John Bradley, Jr. and VC-15 dated September 3, 2019.

E-mail from Nathaniel Patch, Archivist, Archives II Reference Section (RDT2) National Archives at College Park, MD to the author on August 27, 2019.

Ford Motor Company Eagle Boat blueprints, diagrams and technical specifications, Henry Ford Museum, Dearborn, Michigan.

Formerly Classified April 24 & 25, 1945 Action Reports, Deck Log Entries, Antisubmarine Action by Surface Ship Reports, Depth-Charge & Hedgehog Attack Plots and War Diary of U.S.C.G.C. *92004*.

Formerly Classified April 24 & 25, 1945 Action Reports, Deck Log Entries, Antisubmarine Action by Surface Ship Reports, Depth-Charge & Hedgehog Attack Plots and War Diary of U.S.S. *Muskegon* (*PF-24*).

Formerly Classified April 23, 1945 Action Reports and Deck Log Entries of U.S.S. *Craven* (*DD-382*).

Formerly Classified April 23, 1945 Action Reports and Deck Log Entries of U.S.S. *Earle* (*DD-635*).

Formerly Classified April 23, 1945 Action Reports and Deck Log Entries of U.S.S. *Evarts* (*DE-5*).

Formerly Classified April 23, 1945 Action Reports and Deck Log Entries of U.S.S. *Tenacity* (*PG-71*).

Formerly Classified April 23, 1945 Action Reports and Deck Log Entries of U.S.S. *Woolsey* (*DD-437*).

Formerly Classified April 23, 1945 Action Reports, Deck Log Entries, Report on Sinking of USS *Eagle 56* and Rescue Operations, Antisubmarine Action Report and Depth-Charge Attack Plot of U.S.S. *Selfridge* (*DD-357*).

Formerly Classified Correspondence Files of the Secretary of the Navy/Chief of Naval Operations (Record Group 80), JAG:I:CP:nrc (SC)LII-I/PE56 Doc.#169311.

Formerly Classified May 7, 1945 Deck Log Entries of U.S.S. *Acme* (*AMc-61*).

Formerly Classified Eastern Sea Frontier Activity Report of 29 April 1945;

Formerly Classified May 5/6, 1945 Action Reports, Deck Log Entries, Antisubmarine Action Report, and Depth-Charge & Hedgehog Attack Plot of U.S.S. *Atherton* (*DE-169*).

Formerly Classified May 5/6, 1945 Action Reports and Deck Log Entries of U.S.S. *Ericsson* (*DD-440*).

Formerly Classified Non-Submarine Contacts: Western Atlantic and Caribbean Sea. U.S. Naval Oceanographic Office, Second Edition, 1968.

Formerly Classified U.S. Navy COMINCH "Ultra" Sub-Tracking Room "Op20G" Enigma decrypt logs, April 1945.

Formerly Classified "Functions of the "Secret Room" (F-211) of COMINCH Combat Intelligence, Atlantic Section Anti-Submarine Warfare, WWII" (Undated).

Formerly Classified Commander Eastern Sea Frontier: War Diary Eastern Sea Frontier: Activity Prior 24 April 1945 (RE: EAD 1215/23) COMINCH evaluation. 1945.

Formerly Confidential Extract from Deck Log of U.S.S. *Nantucket* (*LV-112*). Monday, April 23, 1945.

Formerly Confidential letter of Felix Gygax, (USN) Rear Admiral, Commandant, First Naval District and Navy Yard, Boston, Massachusetts. April 23, 1945.

Formerly Confidential letter of Felix Gygax, (USN) Rear Admiral, Commandant, First Naval District and Navy Yard, Boston, Massachusetts. June 1, 1945.

Formerly Confidential U.S. Coast Guard "operations" section of the First Naval District's War Diary 16 to 30 April 1945.

Formerly Confidential U.S. Navy Court of Inquiry: Loss of U.S.S. *Eagle 56* (*PE-56*), Argument of the Judge Advocate, Findings of Fact & Opinion. June 1, 1945.

Formerly Confidential U.S. Navy Record of Proceedings of Court of Inquiry: Loss of U.S.S. *Eagle 56* (*PE-56*).

Formerly Secret Eastern Sea Frontier, Surface Control Log "Flag File" Records of Naval Operating Forces, May 1945.

Formerly Secret ComDesLant secret dispatch 231751 of April 1945.

Formerly Secret COMINCH File of Messages on U-Boat Estimates and Situation Reports (SRMN-033) 1945.

Formerly Secret COMINCH File: U-Boat Intelligence Summaries January 1943-May 1945 (SRMN-037)

Letter of Admiral, James Forestall, Secretary of the Navy, Washington, D.C. August 29, 1945.

Letter of Captain, A. E. Stone, ChC (USN), District Chaplain, Headquarters First Naval District. May 9, 1945.

Letter of Captain H. G. Patrick, USN (RET.) Navy Dept. Board of Decorations & Medals, to Lt. (jg) John P. Scagnelli. April 3, 1946.

Letter of the Director of Naval History, via the Office of the Chief of Naval Operations, for the Correction of Naval History and the posthumous issuance of Purple Heart Medals to the casualties of the U.S.S. *Eagle 56*, signed by the Secretary of the Navy, Gordon England on June 26, 2001.

Letter of Edwin Walker, "*PE56* Witness," former crewman aboard U.S.S. *Selfridge* (*DD-357*). February 3, 2002.

Letter of E.M. Ellis, Commander (USN), U.S. Naval Air Station: Brunswick, Maine. April 26, 1945.

Letter of J. Wandres to Harry Cooper of Sharkhunters International, dated April 15, 1988.

Letter of Lieutenant, W.J. McNicol, Jr. (USNR), Naval Department: Bureau of Naval Personnel. May 22, 1945.

Letter of Lieutenant (jg), John P. Scagnelli, Jr. (USNR), Surviving Senior Officer of *PE-56*. August 2, 1945.

Letter of Oliver Littleton, former Ensign & Commander of the coastal minesweeper *AMc-61*. April 18, 2003.

Letter of Richard I. DuBurg, former sonarman aboard U.S.C.G.C. *Moberly* (*PF-63*). September 9, 2001.

Letter of Robert L. Ferree, Helmsman U.S.S. *Selfridge*, April 4, 1995.

Letters of Robert W. Scott, Chaplain (USNR), U.S. Naval Air Station: Brunswick, Maine. May 11, 1945.

Letter of Thomas V. Welch, former crewman aboard U.S.S. *Selfridge* (*DD-357*).

Letter of William N. Heckendorf, former aircrewman aboard a PBY5A "Catalina" flying boat of patrol squadron VPB92 out of Quonset Point (RI) Naval Air Station, March 2003.

S.S. *Black Point*: Crew List and Cargo Manifest, Sprague Steamship Co., Boston, MA, May 1945.

State of Maine: Proclamation by Governor, Angus S. King, Jr., A Day in Honor of the Officers and Men of the U.S.S. *Selfridge*. October 21, 1995.

Sworn Affidavit of John L. Breeze, given on December 28, 1998.

Sworn Statement of Alice (Heyd) Hultgren, Y1C, stenographer at Court of Inquiry, given on October 5, 1998.

Sworn Statement of Arthur Gay, former crewman aboard from U.S.S. *Nantucket* (*LV-112*). July 2000.

Sworn Statement of Harold H. Petersen, survivor from *PE-56* given on June 12, 2000.

Sworn Statement of John L. Breeze, survivor from *PE-56*, given on October 5, 1998.

U.S. Coast Guard World War II Memoirs, by Richard I. DuBurg (date unknown).

Western Union Telegram of Vice Admiral, Randall Jacobs, Chief of
     Naval Personnel. August 2, 1945.

NOTE

Please excuse the occasional grammatical and misspelling errors
in the foregoing document, as this is not a final draft. This story is
still being researched, and is updated periodically as new witnesses
are located and interviewed, and as new documentation and evidence
is uncovered. As a result, please check the revised copyright dates to
insure that you have an updated copy. All misspellings, grammatical
errors, and historical inaccuracies from official government records
and other cited sources have been set forth in this account, verbatim.
Every effort has been made to make note of those errors, and to set
forth the appropriate corrections.

Copyright Warning

Researched & Prepared by Author:

Paul M. Lawton, Esquire

Naval Historian

The Lawyers' Building

157 Belmont Street

Brockton, MA 02301-5107

United States of America

(508) 580-8300 Phone

(508) 584-8524 Fax

E-Mail: paulmlawton@yahoo.com